GEORGIA
Off the Beaten Path

GEORGIA
Off the Beaten Path

by **William Schemmel**

A Voyager Book

Chester, Connecticut

Library of Congress Cataloging-in-Publication Data

Schemmel, William.
    Georgia : off the beaten path / by William Schemmel. — 1st ed.
      p.   cm.
   "A Voyager book."
   Includes index.
   ISBN 0-87106-618-1
   1. Georgia—Description and travel—1981- —Guide-books.
I. Title.
F284.3.S34 1989   88-34058
917.58'0443—dc19   CIP

Cover illustration by Pamela Hopson
Text illustration by Carol Drong
Composition and maps by TRG, North Branford, Connecticut

Manufactured in the United States of America
First Edition/First Printing

To my faithful companions,
Freda and Rabun,
who have seen me through
many pleasant journeys.

Northwest

Northeast

Metro
Atlanta

Middle

Southwest

Southeast

Coastal

Contents

Owens-Thomas House, Savannah

Introduction

After spending a good deal of my life wandering Georgia's by-ways, I'm happily convinced it will never run out of ways to surprise and delight me. From the Blue Ridge Mountains by the Tennessee and Carolina borders to the Okefenokee Swamp and piny woods bordering Florida, from Savannah and "The Golden Isles" on the Atlantic Coast to Columbus and La Grange and Lake Seminole on the westerly Chattahoochee River, I'm ever amazed at my home state's depth and breadth. It's like an incredible attic stacked floor to ceiling with a never-ending cache of treasures.

I've attended Sunday morning services with Macon County's Mennonites and been transported by the Gregorian chants of the Benedictine monks at Rockdale County's Monastery of the Holy Ghost. I've awakened in the depths of the swamps to the eerie symphony of gators and owls and at sunrise by mountain lakes to the siren song of loons and geese.

I've encountered ghosts, and tales of ghosts, in antebellum mansions where Sherman and Lafayette once slept and half-believed the outrageous lies of fishermen and small-town sages. I've attended festivals exalting rattlesnakes, chitterlings, sorghum syrup, pecans, autumn leaves, spring dogwoods, and Greek, Chinese, Middle Eastern, East Indian, and American Indian heritage. Along the way, I've eaten a fair share of barbecue, catfish, and fried chicken, as well as accomplished European cuisine, in mountain valleys and small-town cafés.

I've beheld a likeness of the Roman she-wolf nursing Romulus and Remus, donated to an embarrassed small town by Benito Mussolini, and best of all, I've met Georgia's proudest monument, her own people, in their natural habitat. A few grouches notwithstanding, they're warm, wise, witty, and when you wander off the beaten path, they'll be tickled to point you in some fascinating directions.

I hope you'll enjoy using this book half as much as I've enjoyed researching it. When you discover some off-the-beaten-path adventures that I've yet to come across, please let me know by writing to me c/o The Globe Pequot Press, 138 West Main Street, Chester, CT 06412.

Restaurant cost categories refer to the price of entrées without beverages, desserts, taxes, or tips. Those listed as inexpensive are $5 or less; moderate, between $5 and $10; and expensive, $10 and over.

Introduction

The prices and rates listed in this guidebook were accurate at press time, but I recommend that you call establishments before traveling in order to obtain current information.

Before you head off the beaten path in Georgia, orient yourself with information from these sources. General Information: Georgia Tourist Division, Georgia Department of Industry and Trade, P. O. Box 1776, Atlanta, GA 30301 (404) 656–3590. State Parks and Historic Sites: Georgia Department of Natural Resources, Communications Office, 205 Butler Street, Suite 1258, Atlanta, GA 30334; toll-free in Georgia, (800) 3GA–PARK, toll-free outside Georgia, (800) 5GA–PARK.

Off the Beaten Path in Metro Atlanta

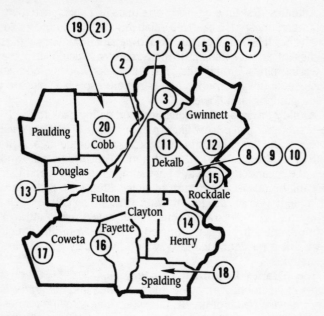

1. Ansley Park/Atlanta Botanical Garden
2. Buckhead neighborhood/Swan House
3. Chattahoochee River National Recreation Area
4. Woodruff Park/CNN Center/Johnny Mercer Room
5. Oakland Cemetery
6. Wren's Nest
7. Center for Puppetry Arts/Ford African Rain Forest
8. De Kalb Farmers Market
9. Emory Museum of Art and Archaeology
10. Stone Mountain Village
11. Chamblee
12. Yellow River Wildlife Game Ranch
13. Sweetwater Creek
14. Panola Mountain State Conservation Park
15. Monastery of the Holy Ghost
16. Mr. Baggarly's Museum/Starr's Mill
17. Powers Crossroads Country Fair & Art Festival
18. Griffin
19. Kennesaw Mountain Battlefield/locomotive General
20. Marietta Town Square
21. Rocky Pine Ranch

Metro Atlanta

Fulton County

Atlanta's first-time visitors are usually flabbergasted by the city's greenness. Thanks to a relatively high altitude—1,050 feet in the foothills of the Blue Ridge Mountains—and about fifty inches of annual rainfall, the city seems to swim in a sea of towering pines, hardwoods, magnolias, dogwoods, and azaleas. Residential neighborhoods and parks are especially blessed with trees, gardens, and flowers.

Ansley Park, a lovely neighborhood dating back to the 1920s, is a soothing place to walk, drive, or ride a bike. On Peachtree Street at the Woodruff Arts Center/Colony Square area, turn east onto 15th Street, then left (north) onto Peachtree Circle, and follow the meandering byways past sumptuous lawns and gardens skirting homes in a spectrum of styles. Stop for a picnic, a walk, or a giddy ride in a swing at Winn Park, at Peachtree Circle and Lafayette Drive. Follow a scenic street called the Prado to Piedmont Avenue. If you get confused by the labyrinthine street pattern, ask a resident for the way out. Even they get lost in here sometimes.

The **Atlanta Botanical Garden,** (404–876–5858), on sixty acres of Piedmont Park at Piedmont Avenue and the Prado, is the city's newest patch of green. Take your time strolling formal gardens and rose gardens, a Japanese garden, and a fifteen-acre hardwood forest with a marked walking trail. Numerous state, regional, and national flower shows are held in the Day Building at the entrance. The Botanical Garden recently opened its showplace and centerpiece. The $5-million Dorothy Chapman Fuqua Conservatory boasts 16,000 square feet of tropical, desert, Mediterranean, and endangered plants. On weekdays from 11:30 A.M. to 1:30 P.M., sandwiches, salads, desserts, and soft drinks are sold in the courtyard of the Day Building. There's also a gift shop, with seeds, bulbs, planters, and how-to books. The Garden is open Monday through Saturday 9:00 A.M. to dusk, Sunday noon to dusk. Adults are $2; senior citizens and ages six to twelve, $1; free for children six and under and for all ages after 1:30 P.M. on Monday.

After visiting the Botanical Garden, you could spend the rest of the day in Piedmont Park. Facilities include tennis courts, a swimming pool, softball fields, playgrounds, and jogging, hiking, and biking paths. Most of the park is closed to auto traffic. Skate Escape (404–892–1292), across from the park at 1086 Piedmont Avenue, will rent you a bike or a pair of roller skates.

The **Buckhead neighborhood,** off Peachtree Street/Road about 6 miles due north of downtown, has long been Atlanta's most splendid residential enclave. West of Peachtree Road, follow the green and white "Scenic Drive" markers past Spanish and Italian villas, French chateaux, Old English Tudors, white-columned Greek Revivals, Georgians, even Japanese-style showplaces that preside over immense lawns and great stands of trees and flowering shrubbery. Some of the most beautiful homes are on West Paces Ferry, Andrews, Habersham, Blackland, Valley, and Tuxedo roads.

For an inside peek at privilege, drop by the Atlanta Historical Society, 3101 Andrews Drive, (404) 261–1837. The feature attraction is **Swan House,** a grand Italianate villa built in the late 1920s by descendants of one of the city's pioneer families. The villa is set off by formal gardens and terraced fountains. European furnishings and art, collected by the Samuel Inman family on their grand tours, fill the large, sunny rooms. Mrs. Inman's beloved swans are the motif of furniture, wall coverings, and artworks throughout the house.

Also on the grounds, the Tullie Smith Plantation hearkens back to simpler times. The 1830s farmhouse and outbuildings are furnished with utilitarian items typical of north Georgia's early years. There are an herb garden, a grape arbor, a gift shop, and a working blacksmith and other craftspeople on special occasions.

McElreath Hall, the Atlanta Historical Society's modern home, displays photographs and memorabilia of the city's heritage. The three areas are open Monday through Saturday 9:00 A.M. to 5:30 P.M.; Sunday, noon to 5:00 P.M. All-inclusive admission is $4.50 for adults, $4 for seniors and students, $2 for those twelve years old and under.

The Georgia Governors Mansion (404–261–1776), near the Historical Society at 391 West Paces Ferry Road, receives visitors Tuesday through Thursday 10:00 to 11:30 A.M. Public rooms in this modern-day Greek Revival mansion, built in the late 1960s, gleam with museum-quality Federal-period antiques and art. Tours are free.

Georgia's nineteenth-century poet Sidney Lanier sang the praises of the Chattahoochee River in his idyllic "Song of the Chattahoochee." The river rises in the north Georgia mountains and flows through metropolitan Atlanta on its way to the Gulf of Mexico.

The **Chattahoochee River National Recreation Area,** a 48-mile stretch of river and gentle rapids flowing between wooded palisades, is the focus for recreational pursuits of all sorts. From spring through fall, Atlantans love to set their rafts, canoes, and kayaks loose in the river for a lazy day of relaxation. Sturdy four-, six-, and eight-person rafts may be rented from Chattahoochee Outdoor Center, 1825 Northridge Road, (404) 395–6851. If rafting isn't your pleasure, you can also spread a picnic, hike, bike, jog, bird-watch, and exercise on the twenty-two-station fitness trail. The park's main entrance is at Highway 41 and the Chattahoochee River bridge. Contact the Park Superintendent, 1900 Northridge Road, Atlanta 30338 (404–394–8139).

The river's fauna and flora is celebrated at the Chattahoochee Nature Center, 9135 Willeo Road in Roswell, (404) 992–2055. The private, nonprofit natural-science center's exhibits of plants and wildlife, special programs, and workshops are in a tranquil fifty-acre setting by the riverbanks, about 25 miles north of downtown Atlanta. Guided walks on Saturday and Sunday at noon and 2:00 P.M. weave through twenty acres of nature trails and a 1,400-foot boardwalk over the river. You can also pick up a brochure and take a self-guided tour. Make a full day of it with a picnic lunch. The center is open daily 9:00 A.M. to 5:00 P.M. Admission for adults is $1; children and senior citizens, 50¢.

Downtown Atlanta's **Woodruff Park** doesn't have a lot of greenery, but on weekdays this open space at Peachtree, Marietta and Decatur streets is an A-1 people-watching location. At weekday lunch, the benches and small patches of grass fill up with Georgia State University students, office workers, street preachers, politicians, free-lance musicians, and entertainers. Pick up a sack lunch at one of the numerous eateries around the park and sit back and watch the show.

Among the downtown area's ultra-modern skyscrapers are some lovely architectural treasures of yesteryear. The William-Oliver Building, on Peachtree Street across from the park, gleams with Art Deco brass elevator doors, ceiling murals, and decorative grillwork. The Candler Building, on the park's northern edge, was built in 1904 by Coca-Cola magnate Asa Candler, who spared no expense in embellishing it with marble friezes, brass and woodwork, and a grand staircase.

The more contemporary **Cable News Network (CNN) Center,** four blocks west of Woodruff Park at Marietta Street and Techwood Drive, is home to media mogul Ted Turner's broadcasting empire. Join tours of the CNN complex, and you may watch your favorite cable news programs being prepared and broadcast live around the world. The 45-minute walking tours (404–827–2300) are highlighted by close-up looks at TBS technicians producing "CNN NEWS" and "CNN Headline News." Memorabilia, photos, and Academy Award Oscars garnered by MGM Studios are also on view (MGM is a part of the Turner family). Tours are conducted Monday through Friday, 10:00 A.M. to 5:00 P.M.; and Saturday and Sunday, 10:00 A.M. to 4:00 P.M. Admission for adults is $4; age 12 and under, senior citizens, and students, $2; age 5 and under, no charge.

Also in the ultra-modern CNN complex are several restaurants and bars, small shops, and a theater that continuously plays *Gone With the Wind.*

GWTW fans may also want to see the memorabilia of the movie and book in the Margaret Mitchell Collection at the Atlanta Public Library, downtown at Carnegie Way and Forsyth and Peachtree Streets (404–577–6940). The movie made its gala 1939 world premiere across the street at Loew's Grand Theatre, where the Georgia-Pacific skyscraper now rises.

One of the most interesting ways to delve into the city's history is on a tour led by the Atlanta Preservation Center. Headquartered in the 1897 Flatiron Building downtown at Peachtree and Broad streets, the center's half-dozen walking tours from April through October focus on the city's architectural and cultural heritage. The Fox Theatre tour takes you backstage of one of America's last surviving 1920s "picture palaces." Adorned with minarets, Moorish arches, Egyptian hieroglyphics, and a blue-sky ceiling that twinkles with electric stars, the Fox (404–881–1977) hosts a full schedule of touring musicals, concerts of all sorts, and a summertime classic movie festival. It's at 660 Peachtree Street at Ponce de Leon Avenue.

And speaking of music, a talented Georgia native son is honored with a small museum at downtown Atlanta's Georgia State University. The **Johnny Mercer Room** at GSU's Library South

Building pays homage to the Savannahian who gave the world "That Old Black Magic," "Come Rain or Come Shine," "Moon River," "Moonlight in Vermont," and dozens and dozens more wonderful tunes. Memorabilia and manuscripts, first-edition sheet music, photos, and other artifacts were donated to the university by Mercer's widow. To get you in the proper frame of mind, a chrome-and-neon jukebox has all of Mercer's favorites. The museum (404–651–2476) is open Monday through Friday 9:00 A.M. to 5:00 P.M. No fee is charged.

Johnny Mercer didn't write "Sentimental Journey," but you can take one on the New Georgia Railroad. Every Saturday, the state-operated NGR hooks a steam locomotive or two to a string of museum-quality passenger and club cars and chugs off for excursions around Atlanta. Trains leave from the entrance of the Underground Atlanta complex at 10 Central Avenue (404–656–3253), near the Zero Mile Post, where Atlanta was born as a railroad terminus in the mid-1830s. Three Saturdays a month, the route is a ninety-minute, 18-mile loop through the city's neighborhoods and historic landmarks; one Saturday a month, the end of the line is Stone Mountain Park and Stone Mountain Village. Both trips are $10 adults; $5 age three to twelve; age two and under no charge.

Nonstop loop trips leave at 10:00 A.M., noon, and 2:00 P.M. On the Stone Mountain run, leaving downtown at 9:00 A.M., noon, and 3:00 P.M., you can get off at the village, have lunch, and browse the many handicraft, antique, and Civil War memorabilia shops along the covered Main Street. You may also ride into the park and climb the great rock. If your group is large enough, you can reserve an entire car for a private party. It's a unique setting for a birthday celebration.

MARTA, the Metropolitan Atlanta Rapid Transit Authority, is a more up-to-date way to get around the city. The clean, luxurious two-line rapid rail system intersects at Five Points Station downtown and is a swift way of getting to the Woodruff Arts Center/High Museum of Art and other attractions. The MARTA bus system is a more comprehensive, but much slower way of getting about. Fare for both is 85¢ one way, including transfers; for information (404) 522–4711.

Oakland Cemetery, 248 Oakland Avenue at Memorial Drive (404–577–8163), is a book on Atlanta's past, right behind the ultra-modern King Memorial MARTA Station. Established in 1850,

Oakland has red brick walls that enclose a wealth of architectural and cultural heritage. Here is buried *Gone With the Wind* author Margaret Mitchell, struck down by a taxi on her beloved Peachtree Street in 1949. Victorian aristocrats are entombed in temple-like mausoleums, embellished with stained glass, gargoyles, and marble busts. You may walk through Confederate and Jewish sections, see the graves of the city's first-born child and other celebrities, and spread a picnic lunch under the magnolia trees. Open daily. Free tours are conducted on weekends.

A MARTA train to West End Station and a bus connection or three-block walk will bring you to the **Wren's Nest,** the Victorian home of Joel Chandler Harris, creator of Br'er Rabbit, Br'er Fox, the Tar Baby, and other delightful critters who roam his 1880s book *Uncle Remus: His Songs and Sayings.* Rooms are filled with furnishings and mementoes of Harris and his family, editions of his book in many languages, and re-creations of his beloved characters. The house got its name when a mother wren decided that Harris's wooden mailbox would be perfect for her brood. The mailbox now has an honored place among the Wren's Nest's treasures. Especially if you have children, try to visit when story-telling sessions are scheduled—usually the last Saturday of the month and during summer weekdays. Wren's Nest, at 1050 Gordon Street, (404) 753–7735, is open Tuesday through Saturday 10:00 A.M. to 5:00 P.M., Sunday 2:00 to 5:00 P.M. Adults are $3; senior citizens and teens $2; ages four to twelve, $1.

Children, as well as adults, will enjoy the Center for Puppetry Arts (404–873–3391), on the northern edge of downtown at 1404 Spring Street. The converted red brick school building houses a fascinating puppetry museum and puts on a year-round program of puppet theatricals, some aimed at youngsters, others tailored for adults.

The **Ford African Rain Forest** at Zoo Atlanta is another treat for all ages. The five-acre natural habitat is the home of "Willie B.," a 450-pound silver-back gorilla from the Congo, and his extended family of fellow primates, who roam freely among the rain forest's trees and grassy hillsides. The zoo's more than 150 species of birds and animals also include Chilean flamingos, polar bears, sea lions, Vietnamese pot-bellied pigs, elephants, big cats, tropical birds, and one of the world's largest reptile collections. Many of the animals are featured in regularly scheduled shows. The zoo is in Grant Park, Georgia and Cherokee avenues, three miles south of downtown, 404-624-5678. Admission for adults is $4.25; ages 3 to 11, $2.25; age 3 and under, no charge. Open daily 10:00 A.M. to 5:00 P.M.

Also in Grant Park, you'll find the Cyclorama (404-658-7625), a dramatic painting 50 feet high and 400 feet in circumference that takes you onto the American battlefield. While you stand on a platform in the center of the painting, a narrator tells a moving account of this crucial hour in the Civil War's Battle of Atlanta. Three-dimensional figures and artillery pieces enhance its realism. Shows start every half hour, 9:30 A.M. to 4:30 P.M. daily. Admission for adults is $3; senior citizens, $2.50; ages 6 to 12, $1.50; age 6 and under, no charge.

Atlanta's cosmopolitan character is reflected in restaurants whose specialties range from traditional Southern cooking to exotic dishes from around the world. The biggest selections of restaurants dear to locals' hearts are in the neighborhoods of Buckhead—around the junction of Peachtree, Roswell, East and West Paces Ferry roads, 6 to 8 miles north of downtown—and Virginia/Highland—a reborn older neighborhood extending from Ponce de Leon Avenue north on North Highland Avenue to Virginia Avenue, about 3 to 4 miles northeast of downtown.

Here are few local favorites:

Ben Chau, a hospitable neighborhood Vietnamese restaurant, serves delicious spring rolls; mussel soup; pork, chicken, beef, and seafood dishes. Brown bag with your own wine and beer. Meals are very inexpensive, and no credit cards are accepted. It's open for lunch and dinner Monday through Saturday at 1821 Piedmont Road, (404) 874–0904.

Burton's Grill, across from the Inman Park MARTA rail station at 1029 Edgewood Avenue, offers world-class soul food in cheerful but humble surroundings. Executives to day laborers line up for Deacon Lyndell Burton's glorious fried chicken, vegetables, corn bread, and cobblers. A full meal will be less than $4, and as the sign says, "The Credit Manager Is Out." Burton's (404–525–3415) serves breakfast and lunch Monday through Friday.

Camille's (404–872–7203) on 1186 North Highland Avenue is an always bustling New York–style Italian café that specializes in bountiful servings of seafood, pasta, veal, and chicken in rich, well-seasoned sauces. In warm weather, take an outdoor table. Prices for dinner Monday through Saturday are moderate, credit cards accepted.

When you feel like dressing up just a little, take a table at Chefs' Café (404–872–2284), an excellent small restaurant with a New American menu highlighted by terrific crab cakes, innovative entrées, soups, and desserts. Prices are inexpensive to moderate at lunch (Tuesday through Friday) and dinner (daily except Monday). Credit cards are accepted. The café is located in LaQuinta Motor Inn on 2115 Piedmont Road.

You'll find The Colonnade, at 1879 Cheshire Bridge Road (404–874–5642), like a nostalgic visit to mom's dinner table. This cherished Atlanta institution serves hearty plates of roast beef, fried chicken, chicken pot pie, fried and broiled seafoods, fresh vegetables, and rib-sticking breakfasts. Prices are inexpensive (no credit cards accepted) for breakfast, lunch, and dinner, served daily.

A busy, brightly lighted Hong Kong–style restaurant in the northeastern suburb of Chamblee—Honto Chinese Restaurant—specializes in delectable fresh seafood dishes, written in Chinese and displayed on the walls. Your waiter can guide you to some memorable experiences. Dungeness crab with ginger and scallion sauce is sensational! There's also a menu written in English. Prices are inexpensive at daily lunch and dinner. Credit cards are accepted. The restaurant is at 2328 Old Stone Mountain Road, off the Buford Highway, (404) 458–8088.

For outstanding steamed and grilled seafood, Bahamian conch fritters, and real Key lime pie, try Indigo, A Coastal Grill, a casual Caribbean–Key West café in the Virginia/Highland neighborhood on 1397 North Highland Avenue (404–876–0676). Prices are moderate, and dinner is served nightly except Monday. Credit cards are accepted. Partners Pantry, next door, is a gourmet take-out, with a large selection of wines, (404) 875–0202.

One of Atlanta's very best ethnic dining rooms, Touch of India—about 3 miles north of downtown at 962 Peachtree Street (404–876–7777)—delights adventurous diners with spicy curry dishes, tandoori chicken, and freshly baked Indian breads. Prices are inexpensive at daily lunch and dinner. Credit cards are accepted.

You can get curb service at your car or walk through the lines inside and enjoy your feast in one of the many TV rooms at the Varsity. An All-American drive-in, in all its neon, enamel, and chrome finery, this revered Atlanta landmark annually serves up tons of chili dogs, super-greasy onion rings and french fries, hamburgers, barbecue, ice cream, and other wondrous cuisine. The

Varsity—very inexpensive, no credit cards—on North Avenue at Interstate 75/85 on the northern edge of downtown (404–881–1706) serves around the clock, seven days a week.

Much of Atlanta's lively and varied nightlife is also concentrated in Buckhead and Virginia/Highland. Consult the *Weekend* tabloid in Saturday's *Atlanta Journal-Constitution* for clubs and performers.

If you'd like to stay in an Atlanta home, contact Bed-and-Breakfast Atlanta, 1801 Piedmont Avenue, Atlanta 30324, (404) 875–0525. Accommodations are in beautiful private homes, and rates usually include a full breakfast and the opportunity to meet Atlantans on an informal basis.

De Kalb County

With a population of more than 500,000, De Kalb is metro Atlanta's second largest county. Amid a patchwork of crowded streets and freeways, shopping malls and subdivisions, you'll find many off-the-beaten-path attractions.

A feast for the senses and one of Atlanta's most international experiences, **De Kalb Farmers Market** in Decatur is a colossal indoor bazaar akin to the great markets of Europe and Latin America. Thousands of square feet are piled high with fresh seafood and meats, cheeses, sausages, breads, spices, pastas, fruits, and vegetables from all corners of the earth. Speaking a Babel of tongues, patrons and clerks are also a mini–United Nations. It's worth the experience, even if you aren't shopping. Open Tuesday through Sunday 10:00 A.M. to 9:00 P.M. Recorded phone messages (404–377–6400) give directions to the market at 3000 Ponce de Leon Avenue. You can also take a MARTA East Line train to Avondale Station.

If you get off the MARTA train at Decatur Station, one stop before Avondale, you'll be in the heart of downtown. Decatur Square in the center of the city of 25,000 preserves a small-town flavor with many small shops and restaurants. Pick up a walking tour map from the De Kalb Historical Society, in the classical-style "old" courthouse (404–373–1088) in the center of the square. Across from the courthouse, Buck's (404–373–7797) is a casually sophisticated place for cocktails, trendy burgers, pastas, chicken and seafood dishes at lunch and dinner daily. Thumbs Up, on 254

West Ponce de Leon Avenue (404–377–5623), is an always busy little diner, with its own unique style of pasta, seafood, sandwiches, and breakfast. It's closed on Mondays.

On the Emory University campus, about 2 miles from downtown Decatur on North Decatur and Oxford roads is the **Emory University Museum of Art and Archaeology** (404–727–7522). This small gem holds a trove of antiquities and modern art. On the first floor, you'll see Greek and Roman coins, amphorae, and an Egyptian mummy with a gilded face. Upstairs are displays of European, American, and Oriental art. The museum is open Tuesday through Saturday 11:00 A.M. to 4:30 P.M.

Across from the campus, you'll find a string of student-oriented shops and eateries such as the popular Everybody's, Jagger's, Moto's, and Lullwater Tavern.

About a mile from the Emory campus, at 156 Heaton Park Drive, is the Fernbank Science Center. Fernbank's focal point is a planetarium with a seventy-foot dome that presents seasonal looks at the galaxies, complete with music and narration. You may scan the real heavens through the Southeast's largest telescope, see exhibits in the natural history museum, walk through nature trails, greenhouses, and botanical gardens. The center is open Monday 8:30 A.M. to 5:00 P.M. and Tuesday through Friday until 10:00 P.M. Hours on Saturday are 10:00 A.M. to 5:00 P.M.; Sunday, 1:00 to 5:00 P.M. Planetarium shows are Tuesday through Friday at 8:00 P.M. and Wednesday, Friday, and Saturday at 3:00 P.M. Planetarium admission is $2 adults, $1 students, under five not admitted. For more information, call (404) 378–4311.

A granite hulk 825 feet high and 6 miles around, with scores of attractions and 6 million yearly visitors, is hardly off the beaten path. However, many Stone Mountain Park visitors miss **Stone Mountain Village.** Outside the state park's gates, the Village's Main Street has a nineteenth-century covered sidewalk and three blocks of stores stocked with old books, Civil War artifacts, handicrafts, geodes, and oddities. You can get a haircut in an old-fashioned barber shop, buy an ice cream, a sandwich, or a full meal. The Old Post Office Country Buffet, on 5379 East Mountain Street (404–469–8950), serves Southern-style chow from a daily lunch and dinner cafeteria line. Take a MARTA bus to the Village from downtown Atlanta or make an adventure of the trip by chugging out on the New Georgia Railroad's steam-powered train (see "Fulton County").

Antique lovers and fellow junkers can have a ball in a big assortment of shops clustered in the northeast De Kalb County town of **Chamblee.** Take MARTA's North Line train to the Chamblee Station and walk two blocks north on Peachtree Road. Around the Peachtree Road/Broad Street junction, explore such fun emporiums as the Paper Chicken (404–458–3010); Moose Breath Trading Co. (404–455–0518); Broad Street Antique Mall (404–458–6316); and the Whippoorwill Co. (404–455–8357). Keep up your strength with cookies, breads, and pastries from LaPetite Bakery, a doll-sized shop across from the post office (404–457–4002).

Gwinnett County

Yellow River Wildlife Game Ranch is a peaceful place in the woods, in the midst of south Gwinnett County's suburban explosion. Just off very busy Highway 78, 3 miles east of Stone Mountain Park, the twenty-four-acre privately owned nature preserve is home for dozens of free-roaming brown deer, huggable bunnies, goats, sheep, coyotes, ducks and geese, pigs and porcupines, foxes, wolves, donkeys, a skunk named William T. Sherman, and a spring-forecasting groundhog named Robert E. Lee.

Deer are Yellow River's self-appointed reception committee. You're no sooner on the tree-shaded walking trail than whole families of gentle does, bucks, and fawns are ambling up for handouts of bread and crackers and a scratch behind the ears. During summer, fragile newborn fawns are an especially appealing sight. Lambs, piglets, baby ducks, and goat kids are also very much in the spotlight.

Small children get a big kick out of the Bunnie Burrows, an enclosed area where rabbits of all sizes and colors seem to enjoy being petted and hand-fed raw carrots and celery.

What's purportedly the largest herd of American buffalo east of the Mississippi roams a back meadow. Black bear, bobcats, mountain lions, foxes, and wolves are secured in open-air enclosures, out of reach of little fingers. If you spread a picnic lunch in a grove by the Yellow River, expect some "deer" friends to drop by for a treat.

You may reserve Yellow River's Birthday House for your youngster's special day or for a family reunion or other group activity.

Yellow River Wildlife Game Ranch, at 4525 Interstate 78 in Lilburn (404–972–6643) is open daily Memorial Day to Labor Day 9:30 A.M. to dusk; the rest of the year, 9:30 A.M. to 5:30 P.M. Admission for adults is $3.50; ages three to eleven, $2.50; two and under, no charge.

Douglas County

Since 1968, the picturesque rapids of **Sweetwater Creek** and the adjacent hardwood and piny woodlands have been the heart of a peaceful day-use state park. A short drive off Interstate 20, 25 miles west of downtown Atlanta, the park serves the populace of rapidly growing Douglas County and many others who find it a delightful retreat from the hurly-burly of big-city life.

The ghostly ruins of the New Manchester Manufacturing Company, a Civil War–era enterprise torched by General William T. Sherman's troops, stands by the churning rapids, which provided the company with power to produce uniforms for the Confederate army. During summer, kick off your shoes and join others wading in the swift, cool waters. Be careful of the slick patches of moss covering the rocks.

Five miles of nature trails lead you through the woods, beside the creek. A 250-acre reservoir is stocked with bass, catfish, and bream, which you can fry in a pan and serve on one of the park's picnic tables. The park is open daily from 8:00 A.M. to sundown. Contact the superintendent, Lithia Springs 30057, (404) 944–1700.

Henry County

Twenty miles southeast of downtown Atlanta, via Highway 155, **Panola Mountain State Conservation Park** is a peaceful 585-acre day-use park, where you may have a walk in the woods, enjoy a picnic, and wonder at a 100-acre granite outcropping that's been part of the Henry County landscape for about a million years. The lichen-covered monadnock is part of a major belt of granite, most dramatically evidenced by Stone Mountain, a few miles away.

Stop first at the park's Nature Center for information on trails leading through the woodlands and around the mountain. Meandering through hardwood and pine forests, the 1¼-mile Microwatershed Trail is a moderately strenuous course. Several stations along the way have benches and markers describing the park's fauna and flora. At the base of Panola Mountain, a three-acre pond is alive with turtles, frogs, fish, and small reptiles.

The ¾-mile Rock Outcrop Trail takes you through the woods to an overlook on one of the mountain's major outcroppings. On Saturday and Sunday afternoons, park naturalists conduct walks and give talks at the small amphitheater near the Nature Center. Picnic tables are located near rest rooms and soft drink machines. Pets on leashes may be walked in the picnic area but aren't allowed on the nature trails.

The park is open daily from 8 A.M. to sundown. Contact the superintendent, Stockbridge 30281, (404) 474–2914.

South of the park, via Highway 155, you'll find small cafés and shops around the pretty little courthouse square in McDonough. On the third Saturday of May, the Geranium Festival fills the square with arts, crafts, and entertainment. The popular Indian Springs State Park is a short drive south of McDonough (see "Butts County").

Rockdale County

Amid the burgeoning suburbs of Rockdale County, a short drive off the busy lanes of Interstate 20, about 25 miles east of downtown Atlanta, the **Monastery of the Holy Ghost** is a place of inordinate peacefulness. Since the late 1940s, Benedictine Trappist monks have dwelt and prayed in this cloistered sanctuary at 2625 Highway 212 in Conyers (404–483–8705). The Spanish Gothic–style buildings, even the stained glass in the main church, are all products of their labors.

Men and women may attend Sunday morning mass in the church, which is highlighted by the monks' chants and prayers. Men may make retreats at the modern guest house nearby. A small shop sells bread, cheese, jam, religious items, and produce and herbs grown in the monastery's fields. You may also bring a picnic lunch to tables that sit by a lake beside the cloister.

The abbey does not observe a strict rule of silence, and most monks may converse with visitors.

Coweta and Fayette Counties

Senoia, a drowsy little Coweta County town on Highway 85, 40 miles south of Atlanta, is like a delightful trip through Norman Rockwell–land. As you're strolling down Main Street, townsfolk smile and inquire politely about your family and your health.

To get the inside scoop on Senoia's past and present, drop by **Mr. Baggarly's Museum,** right on Main Street. This wondrous time capsule was put together by a lively gentleman named James Baggarly Sr. in a turn-of-the-century building that was originally a buggy and wagon store, then a Coca-Cola bottling plant. Mr. Baggarly's collection includes a 1925 Ford Model T and a 1930 Ford Model A, which Mr. Baggarly drove on his rounds as Senoia's postal carrier. He'll also put one of his original quarter-inch Edison phonograph records on his Edison disc phonograph and play a little tune on a vintage upright piano. He's got stacks of photos of graduating classes, church groups, politicians, and locals who've made up the *dramatis personae* of the town for the past century. The museum's mementoes are all wonderful, but meeting and chatting with Mr. Baggarly is the biggest treasure of all. Your appreciation is the only admission fee. He keeps irregular hours, so before you come, call him at (404) 599-6624, or knock on his door, just around the corner on Baggarly Way.

Also on Main Street, Hutchinson Hardware is another revered Senoia institution of long standing. Painted bright blue, with a parade of tall arched windows and doors, the building started out as a Ford dealership in the 1920s and became a hardware store early in World War II, when the Hutchinson's supply of Fords went dry. The aisles are stacked with anything you'd want for fishing, hunting, canning, serious farming and hobby gardening, or building a house or barn and keeping them in proper order. Owner Jimmy Hutchinson is used to hearing townspeople say: "I know what I need is in here somewhere" and "If Hutchinson aint got it, I don't need it."

Senoia has two beguiling places to spend the night. The Culpepper House dates back to 1871, when it was built by Dr. John Addy, a returning Civil War veteran. Mary Brown has ruled the Steamboat Victorian House (404–599–8182) with grace and southern charm since 1982. Four guest rooms, two with private baths, are furnished with Victorian antiques. Public areas shine with gingerbread trim, stained glass, and pocket doors. A full

15

southern breakfast served in the stone-hearthed kitchen is included in rates of $55 double with private bath, $50 with shared bath. Write to Mary Brown at Box 462, Senoia 30276.

The Veranda Inn (404-599-3905), built as a hotel at the turn of the century, was one of the first places hereabouts to be electrified. Now operated by Bobby and Jan Boal, the Veranda sleeps up to sixteen guests in rooms blessedly free of televisions and telephones. For entertainment, guests step onto the spacious front veranda and avail themselves of rocking chairs and a porch swing. A double room with private bath is $65 and comes with a whopping big southern breakfast. The mailing address is simply The Veranda, Senoia 30276.

Four miles north of Senoia, at the junction of Highways 85 and 74, stands **Starr's Mill,** one of Georgia's most photographed landmarks. One look at the 200-year-old red frame mill, hard by a pond and waterfall, and you'll be rushing for your camera, too. When you go, be sure to bring along a blanket and picnic.

Melear's (404-461-7180), on Highway 85 at Fayetteville's southern limits, has been serving delicious barbecue and Brunswick stew for over thirty years. A big plateful costs under $5. During the short wait, amuse yourselves with the owner's collection of pig pottery and portraits. Open for lunch and dinner Monday through Saturday.

Newnan, the Coweta County seat (Interstate 85 and Highway 29), also boasts a grand old courthouse and a regal parade of antebellum mansions. Park your car by the courthouse and take a stroll around the pleasant city of 12,000. You may also enjoy a self-guided driving tour with a brochure from the Newnan/Coweta County Chamber of Commerce, 1 Savannah Street, Newnan 30264, (404) 253-2270.

At lunchtime, locals head for Sprayberry's Barbecue (404-253-4421) off Interstate 85 at exit 9.

During Labor Day weekend, legions of fun-seekers head for the **Powers Crossroads Country Fair and Art Festival,** (404-253-2011), 10 miles west of Newnan on Highway 34. This weekend extravaganza attracts hundreds of craftspeople and artists, clog dancers and bluegrass singers, marching bands, and country chefs.

Spalding County

Bargain lovers should put the Spalding County seat of **Griffin** high on their shopping lists. The textile town of 20,000, on Highways 19/41, 40 miles south of Atlanta, has some especially tempting values in towels and socks.

Dundee Towel Shop (404-227-5581) is an attractive, modern outlet for Dundee corporation's products. First-run and irregular bath towels, beach towels, kitchen towels, *et. al.*, are available in a big variety of styles, colors, and fabrics at prices much lower than you'll find at retail stores. The shop is open Monday through Saturday 9:00 A.M. to 6:00 P.M. Major credit cards accepted. 1440 North Expressway, Griffin 30223.

Spalding Knitting Mills Sock Shop (404-227-4362) has the answer to virtually all your hosiery needs. Aisles are jammed with colorful argyles, athletic socks, dress socks, heavy-duty work socks, as well as pantyhose, sweat shirts and other items made by major manufacturers. Irregulars, with all but impossible to discern blemishes, go for at least half the price you'd normally pay. First-run items are more expensive, but still very much a bargain. It's open Monday through Saturday 8:30 A.M. to 5:30 P.M. No credit cards accepted. On East Broad Street, across from the red-brick Spalding Mills, a block from the center of town. Write, P.O. Box 593, Griffin 30223.

Cobb County

With 450,000 residents, affluent Cobb is one of the nation's fastest growing counties and the northwest flagship of the Atlanta metropolitan area. Off the well-beaten paths of freeways, around the corner from high-rise hotels, glitzy shopping galleries, and trendy eateries, you'll find fascinating historic sites, charming town squares, and outdoor recreation.

After the fall of Chattanooga in late 1863, the Confederates grudgingly fell back to Kennesaw Mountain, 25 miles north of Atlanta and the site of **Kennesaw Mountain National Battlefield Park.** For two weeks of June 1864, 60,000 soldiers dug into the wooded flanks of the 1,808-foot mountain. When a series of assaults failed to dislodge the Southerners, Union commander General William T. Sherman executed a flanking strategy, which forced the Confederates to leave the mountain and retreat to Atlanta.

Stop first at the National Park Service Visitors Center and view the slide presentation and exhibits. Outside are some of the cannons that took part in the battle. From Monday through Friday, you may drive your car up a paved road to a parking area 200 yards below the summit. From there, take an easy walk through the woods studded with cannons, earthworks, and markers telling the story of the battle. On Saturday and Sunday, the mountain road is open only to a free shuttle bus that makes the trip every half hour. In fair weather, many visitors hike at least one way on an easy one-mile trail. If you've the stamina, you can extend your hike from the Kennesaw summit 4 miles to Cheatham Hill and 7 miles to Kolb's Farm, other principal battlegrounds in the Kennesaw theater. The two areas are also accessible by car.

Picnic tables, grills, and rest rooms are in a grove of trees near the visitors center parking area. The park, about $4^1/2$ miles west of Interstate 75's exit 116, is open Monday through Friday 8:30 A.M. to 5:00 P.M.; Saturday and Sunday, to 6:00 P.M. Contact the superintendent, P.O. Box 1167, Marietta 30061, (404) 427–4686.

The **locomotive General** is another tangible souvenir of the Civil War. On April 12, 1862, Union raiders stole the locomotive as it sat in the Kennesaw depot. Their plan to decimate Confederate rail lines as they drove north to Chattanooga was foiled after a 100-mile chase. Eight of the raiders were hanged; the adventure was dramatized in the Disney movie *The Great Locomotive Chase.* The General is now permanently parked in the Big Shanty Museum in the small town of Kennesaw, $3^1/2$ miles from Kennesaw Mountain. You may also see a twelve-minute slide show and Civil War weapons and artifacts. It's open daily. Admission for adults is $2; children, 50¢. Before leaving town, browse through the piles of weapons, uniforms, old photos, and books at Wildman's Civil War Surplus Store, across from the museum. It's run by Civil War enthusiast "Wildman" Dent Myers.

Marietta Town Square, officially called Glover Park, is a charming nineteenth-century microcosm of mellow brick buildings, shady streets, and gingerbread Victorian homes. The grassy park in the center of the square has been landscaped as a restful Victorian green, with a gazebo, playground, a fountain, and plenty of benches for quiet relaxation. Shops around the square are stocked with antiques, art and handicrafts, jewelry and apparel. The square also boasts several good restaurants. The most popular include Schillings on the Square, (404) 428–9520; The Brickworks, (404) 426–0544; and Waterstreet Café (404) 424–6949.

Stop first at the Marietta Welcome Center, in the restored Western & Atlantic Railway Depot just off the square (404–429–1115), for information and directions for a walking tour of the city's lovely antebellum and Victorian neighborhoods. You can stay in a charming bed and breakfast by contacting Victorian Inns of Marietta/Atlanta, 192 Church Street, Marietta 30060, (404) 426–1887. To get to the Marietta square from Highway 41, go west on Roswell Street about 1 mile from the Big Chicken, a local landmark.

Smack in the midst of Cobb County's burgeoning suburbia, **Rocky Pine Ranch**—1231 Shallowford Road, Marietta 30066, (404) 926–3795—is like a little corner of the Old West, offering you the opportunity to trail ride over seventy-five acres of woodlands and rolling countryside. You can hire a horse by the hour, completely outfitted for Western-style riding. And don't worry about a guide, the horses know every inch of the terrain. Twilight rides are followed by square dancing and a hearty steak and potatoes supper. You can also get a group together for a hay ride and during summer come out to the ranch for a rodeo.

When Georgia's summer heat and humidity get you down, take a refreshing plunge into the Atlanta Ocean, a big, boisterous wave pool at White Water Park (404–424–WAVE), on Highway 41 at Marietta. Open daily from May through August, the park has more than thirty attractions: the Ocean, a 750,000-gallon pool that whips up four-foot waves; a variety of water slides; and special areas for the small fry.

For other water-oriented recreation, try Lake Allatoona, which borders Cobb County on the north (see "Bartow County"), and the Chattahoochee River, which Cobb shares on the south with Fulton County and Atlanta.

Off the Beaten Path in Southwest Georgia

1. Bellevue Mansion
2. Chattahoochee Valley Art Association
3. Little White House/Franklin D. Roosevelt State Park
4. Day Butterfly Center/Callaway Gardens
5. National Infantry Museum
6. Columbus Museum
7. American Camellia Society Gardens
8. France Gift
9. Montezuma
10. Andersonville National Cemetery and Historic Site/Andersonville
11. Americus/Plains
12. Providence Canyon State Park
13. Westville
14. Georgia Veterans Memorial State Park
15. Chehaw Wild Animal Park/Thronateeska Heritage Foundation
16. Georgia Agrirama
17. Kolomoki Mounds State Historic Park
18. Fletcher Henderson Jr. Jazz Festival
19. The Mayhaw Tree, Inc.
20. Lake Seminole
21. Climax Swine Time/Rattlesnake Roundup
22. Lapham Patterson House
23. Pebble Hill Plantation
24. Rose Test Gardens

Southwest Georgia

Troup County

La Grange, a pretty town of 25,000 near the Georgia-Alabama border, was named in honor of the Marquis de Lafayette's French estate, which accounts for the bronze likeness of the Marquis in the center of downtown Lafayette Square. Away from the square, regal white-columned mansions preside over well-tended lawns, gardens, and tree-shaded streets.

Bellevue Mansion, 204 Ben Hill Street, (404) 884–1832, was the stately Greek Revival home of U.S. Senator and acclaimed orator Benjamin Harvey Hill. Built in the early 1850s, the home is an architectural treasure inside and out, filled with magnificent furnishings and artworks. It's the La Grange area's favorite wedding venue. Open Tuesday through Saturday, 10:00 A.M. to noon and 2:00 to 5:00 P.M., Bellevue charges an admission fee of $1.50.

Lamar Dodd Art Center (404–882–2911), on the neighboring La Grange College campus, is a strikingly modern museum displaying changing regional and national exhibitions and a permanent collection of American Indian art. It is open Monday through Friday, 10:00 A.M. to 4:00 P.M.; Saturday and Sunday, 1:00 to 4:00 P.M.

The **Chattahoochee Valley Art Association** (404–882–3267), near Lafayette Square at 112 Hines Street, displays paintings, sculpture, and decorative arts in a restored 1890s jail building. It's open Monday through Friday 9:00 A.M. to 5:00 P.M., Saturday until 1:00 P.M.

La Grange celebrates the coming of spring with its mid-May Affair on the Square, a weekend of arts, crafts, and parades. The city has some very nice dining places. In Clover, 205 Broad Street (404–882–0883), is a handsomely restored Queen Anne–style Victorian mansion, which serves beef Wellington, seafoods, soups, salads, and quiche. The house specialty is Country Captain, a spicy chicken dish favored by President Franklin Roosevelt during his Warm Springs years. It's open for lunch and dinner Monday through Saturday and serves cocktails and wines.

For more casual dining, The Rare Bit, 120 Main Street (404–882–8476), serves salads, soups, sandwiches, pasta, seafood plates in a barnwood-memorabilia decor for lunch and dinner Monday through Saturday.

West Point Lake, a mammoth 26,000-acre inland sea a few minutes from downtown La Grange, offers plenty of opportunities for fishing, boating, swimming, waterskiing, and sunbathing. Contact the West Point Lake Resource Manager, P.O. Box 574, West Point 31833, (404) 645-2937. The lake's commercial outlets include Highland Marina, P.O. Box 1644, La Grange 30241, (404) 882-3437, where you may rent fishing boats and go after the lake's channel catfish and white and largemouth bass. Also at the marina, you may rent a houseboat or stay in a campground or furnished cottage. The lake is a U.S. Army Corps of Engineers impoundment of the Chattahoochee River, which forms most of the Georgia-Alabama border.

Meriwether County

President Franklin Delano Roosevelt left his everlasting imprint on the hills and piny woodlands of Meriwether County. The future president first came to this isolated rural county, 85 miles southwest of Atlanta, in 1924, to immerse his polio-afflicted limbs in the mineral waters of Warm Springs. His **Little White House,** secluded in a wooded grove, became his sanctuary from the monumental pressures of World War II. Now maintained by the Georgia Department of Natural Resources, the comfortable little house remains as he left it, when he died here on April 12, 1945.

In the kitchen, simple dishes, pots and pans, a hand-cranked ice cream churn, and other utensils are neatly stacked. In the woodwork, FDR's cook penciled this touching message: "Daisy Bonner cook the first meal and the last one in this cottage for the President Roosevelt." The four-time president was seated in a living room chair, posing for a portrait, when he was fatally stricken. The unfinished portrait remains on its stand.

From the house, the "Walk of States" leads to the Roosevelt Museum. A twelve-minute film includes segments of home movies showing the president swimming; playing with his Scottie dog Fala; carving the Thanksgiving turkey; and driving about the countryside in his 1938 Ford convertible, equipped with hand controls. (The car, all polished, sits in the garage next to the house.) Also displayed in the museum are glass cases filled with gifts and memorabilia: His wheelchair and jaunty cigarette holder, hundreds of walking canes, and a sweater knitted by First Lady Eleanor Roosevelt.

The Little White House and Roosevelt Museum (404–655–3511) are open daily, except Thanksgiving and Christmas, 9:00 A.M. to 5:00 P.M. Admission for adults is $3; ages six to twelve, $1.50; under six, free. Special observances on April 12 commemorate FDR's extraordinary presidency.

The adjacent village of Warm Springs (population 450) has been revived with visitors in mind. More than two dozen stores along the main street are stocked with antiques, collectibles, and Georgia-made arts and crafts. The Victorian Tea Room (404–655–2319), a 1906 mercantile store, has been turned into a cozy dining room specializing in soups, salads, sandwiches, and Southern home cooking. It's open for lunch Tuesday through Sunday and for dinner Friday only. The Warm Springs pools that initially attracted FDR are no longer open.

Franklin D. Roosevelt State Park, about 5 miles west of Warm Springs, on Highway 190, is ideal for a minivacation. On the wooded crest of Pine Mountain, the 9,480-acre park has a lake for swimming, fishing, and boating; hiking trails; and picturesque picnic spots. Roosevelt's favorite was Dowdell's Knob, with sweeping views of the Pine Mountain Valley. Many of the field-stone buildings in the park were the product of the Depression Era Civilian Conservation Corps. Campsites ($8 a night) have water, electricity, hot showers, and rest rooms. Cottages have fire-places and fully-equipped kitchens for standard state fees of $45 and $55 Sunday through Thursday, $55 and $65 Friday and Saturday. The park office, Box 749, Pine Mountain 31822, (404) 663–4858, is open daily 8:00 A.M. to 5:00 P.M.

Greenville, the Meriwether County seat, on Highway 27 north of Warm Springs, is a small pretty town, with an imposing court-house and several antique shops around the square.

Harris County

Butterflies—thousands of them, in all sizes and colors, from exotic places around the world—are free and on the wing at the **Day Butterfly Center** at Callaway Gardens in Pine Mountain. Opened to visitors in September 1988, America's first such natu-

Callaway Gardens

ral attraction was inspired by similar preserves in Europe and the Orient, with some distinctive Georgia touches. It was named in honor of Cecil Day, late founder of the Days Inns of America motel corporation, and is a year-round, indoor-outdoor experience.

As you walk into an 8,000-square-foot, glass-enclosed "rain forest," you're suddenly caught in clouds of feathery giant swallowtails (*Papilio cresphontes*), Paris peacock swallowtails (*P. paris*), green-banded swallowtails (*P. palinurus*), owl butterflies (*Caligo* sp.), passion flower butterfiles (*Helinconius* sp.), and a rainbow of other iridescent beauties from the Orient, the Andes and South Pacific. Butterflies and tropical birds perch side by side on lush tropical foliage. A waterfall gently spatters. Hummingbirds flit past. Bleeding-heart doves hide in the thick tropical foliage. Indoors, you'll find educational displays and a theater with a film all about the remarkable lives of butterflies.

Outside, the native butterfly garden is cunningly designed to lure homegrown butterflies to **Callaway Gardens.** If you'd like to have your own butterfly center, Callaway's horticulturists will show you how to plant a "tender trap" in your back yard.

While you're at Callaway Gardens, you may also take a driving tour of the 2,500 acres of gardens planted with 700 varieties of azaleas and more than 450 types of holly, mums, mountain laurel, rhododendron, dogwood, and wildflowers. These may be viewed in their natural habitat, along 13 miles of roads and walking trails, and inside the John A. Sibley Horticultural Center, a stunning indoor-outdoor conservatory with pools, cascades, and scores of floral displays that change with the seasons.

Callaway's 14,300 rolling, wooded acres also embrace thirteen lakes for swimming, fishing, boating, and waterskiing. Golfers may play sixty-three picturesque holes and sample from a recreational smorgasbord that includes tennis, skeet shooting, horseback riding, biking, and a summertime big-top circus. A half-dozen restaurants range from candlelight to casual.

Lodgings range from rooms at the Inn (about $65 to $100 double) to deluxe villas and cottages from $75 to $200 and up. Callaway Gardens lies 12 scenic miles from Warm Springs and Franklin D. Roosevelt's Little White House (see "Meriwether County"). Contact Callaway Gardens, Pine Mountain 31822, toll-free (800) 282–8181. The Day Butterfly Center is open daily year-round. Admission of adults $5, ages 6-11 $1, under-6 free includes all Callaway Gardens non-resort areas.

The Wedgwood Bed & Breakfast (404–628–5659), at the Harris County seat of Hamilton, 6 miles south of Callaway Gardens, offers lovely overnight accommodations in an 1845 Greek Revival home. You'll be treated to a full Southern breakfast for your double room rate of $35 to $65. Write P.O. Box 115, Hamilton 31811.

Muscogee County

On the Chattahoochee River, with a population of about 300,000, Columbus is Georgia's second largest city. The downtown historic district is highlighted by many mid–nineteenth-century house museums and the Chattahoochee Promenade, a riverside esplanade with gazebos, benches, and historical markers. You'll also note a wealth of fountains, whose splash has inspired the nickname, "Fountain City."

One of the easiest ways to take in the historic sites is the Historic Columbus Foundation's Heritage Tour. The two-hour, $5 tour leaves the Hilton Hotel Wednesday and Saturday at 10:00 A.M. and includes the home of Dr. John Stith Pemberton, the inventor of Coca-Cola, and the lavish Springer Opera House of 1871, whose boards have resounded to Oscar Wilde, Lily Langtry, Will Rogers, and other immortals.

Home of Fort Benning and the U.S. Infantry, it's fitting that Columbus should be the site of the **National Infantry Museum.** On the Benning reservation, the museum's (404–545–2958) three floors and twelve spacious galleries include more than 6,000 items from the French and Indian War to Grenada. Among them are weapons; field equipment; troops' personal gear; a porthole from the battleship *Maine*; sixteenth-century English armor; the wing of a World War Japanese Zero; ancient Korean and Chinese weapons and armor; and documents signed by twenty presidents. The museum is open Tuesday through Friday, 10:00 A.M. to 4:30 P.M.; Saturday and Sunday, 12:30 to 4:30 P.M.

The Confederate Naval Museum, 101 4th Avenue (404) 327–9298, displays the salvaged remains of the Confederate gunboats *Jackson* and *Chattahoochee.* It's open Tuesday through Saturday 10:00 A.M. to 5:00 P.M., Sunday 2:00 to 5:00 P.M.

The city's newest pride is the handsome new **Columbus Museum,** 1251 Wynnton Road, (404) 322–0400. The three-part museum houses a regional history gallery, a hands-on "discovery" gallery for youngsters, and a fine arts–decorative arts gallery.

Hours are Tuesday through Saturday 10:00 A.M. to 5:00 P.M., Sunday 2:00 to 5:00 P.M.

For upscale dining, try Bludau's Goetchius House, in the historic district at 405 Broadway, (404) 324–4863. The New Orleans–style mansion, circa 1839, serves Creole and Southern dishes at Monday through Friday lunch and dinner Monday through Saturday. Also in the historic district, the Oak Tree Café, 814 1st Avenue, (404) 323–7770, is a very attractive place for casual lunch Monday through Friday, and pasta, seafood, trendy chicken and veal dishes at Friday and Saturday dinner.

Contact Columbus Convention & Visitors Bureau, P.O. Box 2768, Columbus 31902, (404) 322–1613.

Peach County

Peach County leaves little doubt that it's the heart of Georgia's most luscious industry. Traveling on Interstate 75 at night, you can't miss "The Big Peach," an enormous illuminated rendition of the fruit on a hundred-foot-pole at the Byron/Fort Valley exit. During the summer, visitors have plenty of opportunities to go into the orchards and pick their own or to buy fresh peaches at packing houses and roadside stands. The Byron/Fort Valley exit 49 is the northern end of the Andersonville Trail, which leads through Fort Valley to Plains on Highways 49 and 280.

Six miles south of Fort Valley, at the Peach/Macon County line, look for a left turn off Highway 49 into the **American Camellia Society Gardens.** Between November and March, pink and white blossoms in every known variety bloom in the Society's nine-acre gardens. All year round, you're invited into the Society's Williamsburg-style headquarters to admire an astonishing collection of 170 porcelain birds and flowers created in the studios of the late American artist, Edward Marshall Boehm. The pieces are so lifelike they appear to be on the verge of flight. Some were created as gifts-of-state from presidents and kings.

The American Camellia Society, P.O. Box 1217, Fort Valley 31030, (912) 967–2358, has open grounds daily from dawn to dusk; the headquarters building and Boehm collection are open Monday through Friday, 8:30 A.M. to 4:00 P.M.

At **France Gift,** "Frenchocolate Factory," Highway 341 south, Fort Valley 31030, (912) 825–8343, you may watch artisans create exquisite chocolates in the European tradition. Some are wrapped in Georgia's own pecans, peanuts, and peaches and beautifully boxed as gifts.

Macon County

Part of the Andersonville Trail, Macon County is the home of Georgia's largest Mennonite community. You may admire ante-bellum white columns in the small towns of Marshallville and Montezuma.

The Macon County seat and a thriving Mennonite Community, **Montezuma** was named by returning Mexican War veterans—which accounts for the Aztec Loan Co., Aztec Motel, and other enterprises. Nearly one hundred Mennonite families give the little town some of the appearance of the Pennsylvania Dutch country. Drive east of Montezuma on Highway 26 past the neat barns and silos and the contented herds of the Mennonite dairy farmers. Three miles from Montezuma—and 14 miles west of Interstate 75's exit 41—look for a black buggy parked in front of Yoder's Deitsch Haus (912–472–2024), a sparkling clean cafeteria where Mennonites in traditional dress prepare truly admirable Southern cooking, spiced with such Pennsylvania Dutch specialties as shoofly pie and pot roast. Before leaving, stop by the bakery for a sackful of cakes, cookies, breads, and strudels. It's open for break-fast, lunch, and dinner Tuesday through Saturday.

You may pick up a driving tour map from the Macon County Chamber of Commerce, P.O. Box 308, Montezuma 31063, (912) 472–2391.

Sumter County

Sumter County, the epicenter of Georgia's peanut industry, is home of the world's most famous peanut farmer, our thirty-ninth president. The southern anchor of the Andersonville Trail, Sumter is also the site of the Civil War's most notorious prisoner-of-war camp.

These days, all is green and peaceful at the **Andersonville National Cemetery and Historic Site.** Stop first at the Na-tional Park Service Visitors Center to view the film and exhibits, then take the self-guided driving tour.

Built in 1864 as confinement for 10,000 Union prisoners of

war, the 26½-acre stockade soon became a charnel house for upwards of 33,000 captives. With the Confederacy barely able to feed and clothe its own forces, about 12,000 of the Andersonville inmates perished of disease and starvation. As park rangers point out, however, Southern prisoners in the more well-off North often fared no better than the Union prisoners at Andersonville.

After the war, the camp commander, Swiss-born Captain Henry Wirz, was found guilty of war crimes and hanged. The self-guided tour leads you past thousands of graves and impressive memorials erected by states whose sons died here. Tunnels testify to the prisoners' usually failed attempts to escape the horrors.

A granite springhouse marks the site of Providence Spring, which legend says flowed from barren ground in answer to prisoners' prayers.

Across Highway 49, the village of **Andersonville** (population 250) has been returned to its 1860s appearance. At the Train Depot–Welcome Center, you'll be greeted by Peggy Sheppard, a live-wire transplanted from Yonkers, New York. She'll direct you to the village's antique and craft shops, picnic groves, and antebellum churches and homes. The Drummer Boy Museum houses an extensive collection of guns, swords, battle flags, and documents signed by Jefferson Davis and Abraham Lincoln. The village's major yearly happenings are Andersonville Antiques and Civil War Artifacts Fair in early May and Andersonville Historic Fair, in early October, which features battle reenactments and scores of craftsmen and musicians.

Andersonville National Historic Site (912–924–0343), Andersonville 31711, is open daily 8:00 A.M. to 5:00 P.M. Also contact Andersonville Town Council (912–924–2558), at the same address.

JoAnn Davis, congenial hostess at the Merriwood Country Inn in Americus, has a charming country bed and breakfast at Andersonville. Called "A Place Away," the two bedrooms in the comfortable, rustic-looking cottage have private baths, working fireplaces, refrigerators, and coffeemakers. Guest rooms and a sitting room are decorated in kick-off-your-shoes casual country-style. Rates of about $45 double come with a bountiful Southern breakfast. Contact JoAnn Davis, Route 6, Box 50, Americus 37109; (912) 924–4992.

At nearby **Americus,** stop at the Americus/Sumter County Chamber of Commerce on 404 West Lamar Street, (912) 924–

2646, for a driving guide to the historic showplaces around the pleasant city of 20,000. Memorabilia of our thirty-ninth president is displayed at the James Earl Carter Library of Georgia Southwestern College.

Downtown at 116 West Lamar Street, The Cheeseboard, (912–928–3353) is a spiffy spot for salads, soups, cheeses, pastas, sandwiches, seafoods, beer, wine, and take-away gourmet items. Breakfast and lunch are served Monday through Saturday; dinner, Tuesday through Saturday.

The Merriwood Country Inn, Route 6, Box 50, Americus 37109, (912) 924–4992, is one of Georgia's most delightful bed and breakfast establishments. Hospitable JoAnn Davis has three lovely rooms in her main house—$35 single, $45 double, with private bath and full Southern breakfast—and an adjacent log cottage with an iron bed and tub-for-two perfect for honeymoons and anniversaries, $70 for one night, $65 for two or more nights. Out in the country, the Merriwood has a yardful of friendly animals, and a pond for a little fishing.

At the DeSoto Confectionary & Nut Co., 13 miles east of Americus on Highway 280, the area's renowned product is sold in and out of the shell; wrapped in vanilla, chocolate, and peanut butter fudge; peanut brittled, carmelized with corn, and otherwise glorified. The "Nut House" is open Monday through Saturday. They also do a booming mail-order business. Write P.O. Box 72, DeSoto 31743, or call (912) 874–1200.

Nearly a decade after his presidency, Jimmy Carter's humble hometown of **Plains** still attracts visitors from far and near. What they find is a souvenir of America's past, an agrarian village of quiet ways and unassuming people. After stopping at the Georgia Visitors Center on U.S. 280, between Americus and Plains, and the local information center next to the train depot, everybody heads for Cousin Hugh's Antiques, a Main Street emporium that sells everything from roasted peanuts to peanut ashtrays, Amy coloring books, and Carter biographies. When Carter is in town, a notice in the antique shop window invites everyone to his Sunday school class at Maranatha Baptist Church. Visitors may see Brother Billy's former service station and drive swiftly past the Secret Service bastion around the Carter home.

Plains Bed and Breakfast (912-824-7252), P.O. Box 217, Plains 31780, is the Victorian home where Carter's parents spent their early married years. Four guest rooms with private bath are $50 each.

Stewart County

Providence Canyon State Park preserves the scenic beauty of an area often referred to as "Georgia's Little Grand Canyon." More than a dozen canyons in the 1,108-acre park have been chiseled out over the past 150 years by the slow, relentless process of soil erosion. As deep as 150 feet, the canyons offer a geological primer and a stunning visual display of stratified soil layers. Many fascinating formations stand alone in the midst of the canyons.

During spring and fall, those making the easy hike to the canyon floor are rewarded by multicolored wildflowers, which complement the pinks, purples, and whites of the Providence soils. From July to September, the rare plumleaf azalea blooms in shades from light orange to salmon and various tones of red and scarlet.

Stop first at the park's interpretive center (912–838–6202) for an overview. A day-use park, Providence has picnic tables, shelters, and rest rooms. It's on Highway 39C, 7 miles west of Lumpkin, and open daily from 7:00 A.M. to dark.

You may stay overnight and fish and boat in the Chattahoochee River, at Florence Marina State Park, Route 1, Box 36, Omaha 31821, (912) 838–4244. Campgrounds have electricity, water, rest rooms, and showers, $8 a night. Furnished efficiency apartments, sleeping up to five, with kitchenettes, are $35 a night Sunday through Thursday and $45 Friday and Saturday. The park also has a swimming pool, tennis courts, a playground, and small grocery store. The park is on Highway 39C, 10 miles west of Providence Canyon.

If **Westville** were near an interstate highway, more than a million visitors a year would enjoy it. As it is, far from major thoroughfares, at the tiny Stewart County seat of Lumpkin, Georgia's "Village of the 1850s" is appreciated by only a fortunate 50,000 or so. Forty miles southeast of Columbus, twenty-five miles west of Jimmy Carter's Plains, this Williamsburg-style recreation includes more than two dozen authentic nineteenth-century homes, public buildings, and craftsmen's shops, lining the hard-packed clay streets.

As you walk about the town, you'll be treated to a symphony of workaday sounds: the blacksmith hammering nails, horseshoes, farm implements, and household utensils; the cobbler tapping together a pair of fine riding boots; the schoolmarm calling her charges to class. Elsewhere, townsfolk make their own soap, furniture, and candles; hand-stitch quilts; and cook corn bread, stews, and gingerbread over an open hearth. A mule plods in stoic circles, turning an enormous round stone that grinds sugar cane into thick, amber syrup.

Life-styles range from the rich and famous at the Greek Revival McDonald House to the cottages of the working folk. Every season has its special events: the Spring Festival in early April; May Pole Dances, May 1; Early American, July 4; the Fair of the 1850s, late October–early November; and, at Christmas, strolling carolers and Yule Log lighting.

Westville, P.O. Box 1850, Lumpkin 31815, (912) 838–6310, is open Monday through Saturday, 10:00 A.M. to 5:00 P.M.; Sunday, 1:00 to 5:00 P.M. Admission is adults, $3.50; over age sixty-five, $2.50; students, $1.50.

With its red brick courthouse, granite Confederate soldier, and one-story buildings flanking the quiet square, Lumpkin could be moved, intact into a museum as an exhibit of nineteenth-century Americana. The Bedingfield Inn, (912) 838–4201, was built in 1836 as a doctor's residence and stagecoach inn. It's open irregularly, so phone ahead. Also on the square, the Village Square Restaurant (912–838–6400), run by a couple who moved here from San Diego, serves breakfast, lunch, and dinner Monday through Saturday.

Crisp County

Georgia Veterans Memorial State Park is a tranquil haven 9 miles west of Cordele and the racetrack lanes of Interstate 75. A museum and vintage aircraft honor the state's military veterans. The park sits on Lake Blackshear, an 18-mile-long waterway renowned for catfish, black bass, bream, pickerel, and other delicious catches. Visitors may also enjoy boating, swimming in a fresh-water pool, and a nature interpretive center and playground. The one hundred camping and trailer sites have electricity, water, rest rooms, and hot showers for $8 a night. Ten 2- and 3-bedroom cottages, with fireplaces and fully equipped kitchens, are the standard state fees of $45 and $55 Sunday through Thursday, and $55 and $65 Friday and Saturday. The park office on Highway 280, Cordele 31015, (912) 273–2190, is open daily 8:00 A.M. to 5:00 P.M.

Daphne Lodge, on Highway 280 near the park entrance, (912) 273–2596, is a pleasantly rustic, family-owned restaurant famous for its fried catfish and hushpuppies. They also serve shrimp, steaks, and fried chicken at dinner Tuesday through Saturday.

If you're down this way the first week of July, join in the fun of Cordele's annual Watermelon Festival.

Dougherty County

Approaching Albany from any direction, you'll pass symmetrical groves of papershell pecan trees. Pecans are available the year round, still in the paper-thin shell or roasted and boxed. Some groves invite you to come in and pick your own. The attractive city of 75,000 has other pleasant surprises.

At **Chehaw Wild Animal Park,** on Highway 91, 2½ miles northeast of the city, (912) 430–5275, African elephants and giraffes, Andean llamas, North American black bears, bobcats, elk, bison, and deer roam in natural habitats designed by Jim Fowler, former naturalist with TV's "Wild Kingdom." You view the animals from protected elevated walkways. Also in the 586-acre park, you'll find picnic areas, boating, fishing, water skiing, and camping areas. It's open 9:00 A.M. to 6:00 P.M. daily. Admission is $2 per car, $5 per van, $20 for buses; free from Thanksgiving to end of February.

Thronateeska Heritage Foundation, 100 Roosevelt Avenue, (912) 432–6955, is a delightful time-trip through the nineteenth and early twentieth centuries. The complex includes an early 1900s "prairie style" train depot, a 1910 steam locomotive, 1840s house, and a planetarium and science center in a vintage Railway Express Co. office. It's open Tuesday through Sunday 10:00 A.M. to 5:00 P.M.

The Albany Museum of Art, 311 Meadowlark Drive, (912) 439–8400, has permanent and changing displays of regional and national artists. Open Tuesday through Sunday, noon to 5:00 P.M. Admission for adults is $2, students $1, under 12 no charge.

Carr's Steak House, 609 North Slappey Drive, (912) 439–8788, is a favorite place for steaks, seafoods, cocktails, dancing. Lunch and dinner are served Monday through Saturdays. Albanians also prefer the American menus at Han's, 3101 Gillionville Road, (912) 883–1865, and the dining room of the Quality Inn Merry Acres, 1504 Dawson Road, (912) 439–2261. For Southern cooking, they head for Aunt Fannie's Checkered Apron, 826 Byron Road, (912) 888–8416.

Contact Albany Chamber of Commerce, Box 308, Albany 31702, (912) 883–6900.

Tift County

The **Georgia Agrirama** is an off-the-beaten-path experience less than a quarter mile off the well-beaten paths of Interstate 75. About three dozen vintage farm buildings make up the state's agricultural heritage center. Inside the gates of this nineteenth-century time warp, youngsters may go nose-to-nose with friendly farmyard animals and take a trip on a steam-powered logging train. Cotton is planted in the old-fashioned way by a farmer in bib overalls commanding a mule and a plow. The village black-smith hammers out nails and utensils over a white-hot forge. Sugar cane is harvested by hand and ground into syrup, and corn into grits and meal, at a picture-postcard gristmill. A country store sells handmade quilts, preserves, cookbooks, toys, and corn shuck dolls. On Saturday nights between mid-April and mid-October, "The Wiregrass Opry" is a gala open-air revue with clog dancers, bluegrass fiddlers, and gospel singers.

The Agrirama, P.O. Box Q, Tifton 31793, (912) 386–3344, is open from Labor Day through May 31, Monday through Saturday 9:00 A.M. to 5:00 P.M. and Sunday 12:30 to 5:00 P.M.; June 1 to Labor Day, daily 9:00 A.M. to 6:00 P.M. All-inclusive admission is $3 adults; $2.50, sixty-five and over; $1.50, age six to sixteen; no charge, under six. "Wiregrass Opry" is $4 per car.

Early and Randolph Counties

Kolomoki Mounds State Historic Park, Route 1, Blakely 31723, (912) 723–5296, is an important archaeological site, as well as a recreation area. Within the 1,293-acre park you may climb some of the seven burial mounds and temple mounds built by Creek Indians in the twelfth and thirteenth centuries. The small museum has artifacts unearthed from the mounds and the excavated burial mound of a tribal chief. Also in the park, you're invited to swim in two pools, fish and boat in a pair of lakes, have a picnic, and play miniature golf.

The park's thirty-five camping sites ($8 a night) have water and electricity, hot showers and rest rooms.

Driving around the Early County Courthouse in Blakely, look for the monument to the peanut. A more delicious "monument" is nearby. Miss Brown's Busy Bee Café, (912) 723–3588, serves some of the best homecooking in southwest Georgia, and there's always a selection of at least a dozen pies to follow up the fried chicken, catfish, barbecue, and other hearty dishes. Lunch is served Monday through Friday.

Layside Bed and Breakfast, 611 River Street, Blakely 31723, (912) 723–8923, is a lovely inn in the century-old home of Jean-neane and Ted Lay. Rooms with private bath and continental breakfast are $40; $25 and $35 with shared bath.

At nearby Cuthbert, the **Fletcher Henderson Jr. Jazz Festival** in early summer honors a native son (1897–1952) generally recognized as the single most important figure in the development of American big band jazz. Louis Armstrong and Coleman Hawkins were among many who got their start with Henderson's band. The festival brings together college and professional jazz groups, with some really big names—Lionel Hampton appeared at the 1988 festival.

For information contact, Rod Glenn, Cuthbert/Randolph Co. Chamber of Commerce, Box 31, Cuthbert 31740, (912) 732–2683.

Miller County

Every May, in the swamps and bogs of southwest Georgia, a thorny, scrubby, rather homely tree called the mayhaw produces an applelike fruit prized by gourmets and homemakers. The small, coral-hued fruit is first gathered in fishing nets and by hand along the shoreline, then turned into a delectable sweet-tart jelly doled out only on special occasions.

In 1983, four enterprising women in the tiny southwest Georgia town of Colquitt (population 2,000) saw a way to capitalize on the mayhaw's regional celebrity, spread its gospel nationwide, and boosted their hometown's economy. Thus was born **The**

Mayhaw Tree, Inc., a cottage industry that has rapidly made the shy little mayhaw something of a household word in thirty states and Canada.

If you stop by the small plant at Colquitt, you might see one of the founders stirring a batch of jelly on a stove or packaging the jars for mail-order shipment. You can buy an eleven-ounce jar for about $5 or look for it in specialty stores back home.

As a hedge against a mayhaw drought, six other products also wear the Mayhaw Tree label. These include mayhaw syrup, mayhaw port wine jelly, salad dressing with Georgia's sweet Vidalia onions, raisiny ham sauce, and cucumber and pepper jellies. Colquitt is on Highways 27 and 91, 50 miles southwest of Albany. Write The Mayhaw Tree, Inc., P.O. Box 144, Colquitt 31737, (912) 758–3227.

Decatur, Grady and Seminole Counties

If ever a body of water was created with fishermen in mind, it's got to be **Lake Seminole.** And if ever a man was created for a fisherman's lake, it must be Jack Wingate. Formed by an impoundment of the Chattahoochee and Flint rivers, the 37,500 acre-lake, with a 250-mile shoreline, is especially bountiful grounds for bass fishing. Largemouth routinely weigh in at upwards of fifteen pounds. Anglers also snare a wealth of bodacious black bass, white bass, hybrid bass, and stripers, as well as bream, chain pickerel, catfish, yellow perch, and many other varieties.

Yet the marshy, reedy lake—afloat with thousands of acres of grass beds and lily pads, and spiked with the ghostly trunks of cypress and live oak trees—is so far off the beaten path, down where Georgia's southwest corner bumps against Alabama and Florida, that when more than fifty boats appear on a single day, old-timers grumble that "Ol' Sem" is turning into a waterbound Interstate 75.

One of the first persons you'll meet around the lake is Jack Wingate. His Bass Island Campground and Lunker Lodge, Route 1, Box 1571, Bainbridge 31717, (912) 246–0658, is the only commercial fishing camp on this whole vast waterway. Character supreme, raconteur, humorist, tall-tale teller, sometimes newspaper columnist, and walking encyclopedia of anything that has to do with fishing, Wingate grew up in these parts, well before the Jim Woodruff Reservoir flooded the landscape in 1957. He can point to a place, now underwater, where Spanish friars from Cuba established missions in the 1650s and another where Generals Andrew Jackson, Zachary Taylor, and Winfield Scott built a fort in 1816 to attack Seminole and Creek Indians.

With an average depth of nine to twelve feet and in many areas shallow enough for you to stand on the bottom and flycast, these stump-studded waters can rip open an inexperienced boat like an aluminum can. Hence, you'll need the services of Wingate or one of his fellow guides ($100 a day, including fuel, boat, and motor). Some do double-duty as duck-hunting guides, for which Seminole is also renowned. You can engage them at the Lunker Lodge, off Highway 97 south, between Bainbridge and Chattahoochee, Florida.

The Lodge carries complete lines of fishing gear, ice, groceries, and rental boats. The restaurant is worth the trip, even if you're not intending to fish. Festooned with stuffed trophies, Indian arrowheads, World War I helmets and other odds and ends, the rustic dining room specializes in absolutely first-class fried and broiled fish, shrimp, oysters, barbecue, chicken, and hearty Southern breakfast, at very modest prices.

The adjacent Bass Island Campground and Lodge has forty-eight camp sites ($7 a night) and sixteen motel rooms with kitchenettes ($25 double). The Stag Lodge sleeps sixteen men at $6 each. Aspiring young fishermen, between ages eight and fourteen, may want to sign up for Jack Wingate's Boys Camp, a week of fishing, fun, and water sports during the summer.

The lake's other recreational area is Seminole State Park, off Highway 39, sixteen miles south of Donalsonville (912–861–3137). Facilities include fishing, boating, swimming, waterskiing, picnicking, camping ($8 a night), and furnished cottages ($45 a night Sunday through Thursday, $55 Friday and Saturday).

If you're a fan of country fairs and enjoy good, old-fashioned fun, put **Climax Swine Time** (912–246–6560) on your post-Thanksgiving calendar. Held the Friday and Saturday after Thanksgiving, in the Decatur County community of Climax, many of the activities are pig-related: A hog-calling contest, best-dressed pig competition, a greased-pig chase, and a "chitlin" (chitterling) eating contest. Also on the agenda are country and gospel music, a 10-K race, cane grinding and syrup making, and barbecue and fried chicken for those who care not for "chitlins."

The **Rattlesnake Roundup** (912–762–4243), the last week-end of January, is the social event of the year at the small Grady County town of Whigham, 6 miles east of Climax. The event began a couple of decades ago when Whigham residents, tired of being accosted by the hissing reptiles every time they walked through their fields and farms, decided to do something about it and have some sport at the same time. On the big day, visitors pack tiny downtown Whigham as snakes by the hundreds are brought in and displayed.

In nearby Cairo (*kay-ro*), you'll find some nice shops and casual dining at Peacock Place, a Victorian home turned small shopping gallery. The Peacock's Garland Café and Deli (912–377–6204) has a nice selection of salads, sandwiches, and desserts. Open Monday through Saturday, it's located at 80 4th Avenue.

Thomas County

From 1870 to the turn of the new century, Thomasville was a Southern Newport, the forefather of Palm Beach and Miami. Encouraged by reports of the area's healthy climate, wealthy Northerners came by private train to spend the winter at grand hotels, which brought chefs and orchestras all the way from New York and Europe. Many regular visitors built their own lavish homes and purchased surrounding plantations for grouse and quail hunting. In the early 1900s, the rich and famous discovered Florida, and Thomasville's "Golden Age" was over. Left behind was a remarkable heritage. Presidents, aristocrats, and "commoners" still flock to the city of 20,000 to hunt game birds and antiques, tour homes and plantations, and participate in late April's Thomasville Rose Festival.

Stop first at the Thomas County Chamber of Commerce Welcome Center, 401 South Broad Street, Thomasville 31799, (912) 226–9600, for maps and information. A two-hour guided bus tour includes major sites in and around the city. The charge for adults is $5; $3, age six to twelve.

On your own, stop at the Thomas County Historical Museum, 725 North Dawson Street, where you'll see hundreds of photos and souvenirs of the "Golden Age." It's open daily 2:00 to 5:00 P.M. Admission for adults is $2; students, 50¢.

Nearby, the **Lapham-Patterson House,** 626 North Dawson Street, is an outlandish Victorian mansion built for Chicago shoe baron C. W. Lapham. Maintained as a state historical museum, the tri-winged, mustard-yellow mansion is highlighted by cantilevered interior balconies, double-flue chimneys, and fish-scale shingles. It's open Tuesday through Saturday 9:00 A.M. to 5:00 P.M. Sunday 2:00 to 5:00 P.M. Admission is charged: adults, $1, age six to eleven, 50¢.

Pebble Hill Plantation (912-226-2344) is a "must-see." The twenty-eight-room Georgian and Greek Revival main house, the gardens, stables, and kennels were left as a museum by the late Pansy Ireland Poe. Inside the house are thirty-seven original John James Audubon bird prints and extensive collections of silver, crystal, and antique furnishings. Five miles southwest of Thomasville, on Highway 319, it's open Tuesday through Saturday 10:00 A.M. to 5:00 P.M., and Sunday 1:00 to 5:00 P.M. Adult admission fee is $2 grounds, $5 main house; under twelve, $1 grounds, not permitted in main house.

Susina Plantation Inn, Route 3, Box 1010, Thomasville 31792, (912) 377-9644, is your doorway to Old South romance. In this white-columned Greek Revival masterpiece, rooms are furnished with canopy beds, antiques, and all the contemporary conveniences. Rates of $150 a couple per night, $100 single, include a Southern hunt breakfast and a candlelight dinner with wine. You can unwind at the swimming pool and lighted tennis court.

In town, the Neel House, 502 South Broad Street, Thomasville 31792, (912) 228-6000, is a live oak-shaded turn-of-the-century Neoclassical residence turned inn and restaurant. Accommodations include a spacious double at $70 a night and a one-bedroom suite with a porch overlooking a park for $85, including continental breakfast. Three Toms Tavern, a cozy publike dining room in the Neel House cellar, serves lunch and dinner daily and a popular Sunday brunch.

Also downtown on 217 South Broad Street, Plaza (912-226-5153) serves a Greek/American menu of *moussaka*, steaks, seafoods, children's plates, Southern breakfast, cocktails, and wines daily.

Thomasville's really big annual event is the late April Rose Festival, a week of parades, pagaentry, home tours, and rose judgings that attracts visitors from many countries. From April through November, the **Rose Test Gardens,** 1840 Smith Avenue, (912) 226-5568, displays more than 2,000 rose plants, at no admission charge.

Off the Beaten Path in Southeast Georgia

1. New Perry Hotel/Heileman Brewery
2. Chappell's Mill/Bellevue Avenue/Fish Trap Cut
3. Vidalia Sweet Onion
4. Fruit Cake Plant Tours/Rattlesnake Roundup
5. Big Pig Jig
6. Statue of Liberty/Little Ocmulgee State Park
7. The Rocks
8. Lake Grace
9. Suwannee Canal Recreation Area/Stephen C. Foster State Park
10. Okefenokee Swamp Park/Laura S. Walker State Park

Southeast Georgia

Houston County

The **New Perry Hotel** has been a beacon for middle Georgia travelers since the 1920s, when it replaced a circa 1854 country inn. In bygone days, when Highway 41 funneled Florida-bound vacationers through the center of Perry, the New Perry's cheerful guest rooms—and especially its dining room—were a command performance. Even now, with most of the traffic a mile away on Interstate 75, weary motorists still find their way to this surviving vestige of small-town hospitality.

Set among trees and gardens, across from the Houston (*House-ton*) County Courthouse, the New Perry has thirty-seven rooms in its main building and seventeen more in a modern motel-type addition by the swimming pool. They go for a modest $26 to $38 a night. They're nice, comfortable, and air-conditioned, but the dining room is the main attraction.

With its starched white tablecloths, fresh flowers, bird and floral prints, this is the genteel Southern dining room personified. The menu is the chapter-and-verse Sunday Southern dinner: fried chicken, broiled Spanish mackerel and perch, baked ham, turkey and dressing, stewed corn, turnip greens, yams, green beans, congealed salads, shrimp cocktail, pecan and peach pies. Breakfast is also the full Southern board of grits, hot biscuits, sausage, ham, and eggs.

Breakfast, lunch, and dinner are served daily, at prices that are inexpensive by any standard. Breakfast will be about $3, lunch around $4, and dinner with entrée, three vegetables, and chilled relish tray, no more than $6 or $7. No alcohol is served. Contact the New Perry at 800 Main Street, Perry 31069, (912) 987–1000.

The **Heileman Brewery,** on Highway 341, 6 miles southeast of the hotel, (912) 987–3639, offers free tours of its modern plant Monday through Friday. On the drive, you'll pass the pecan groves and peach orchards for which this area is famous. You can take an off-the-beaten-path route to the Georgia coast by continuing on Highway 341 through Hawkinsville, McRae, Hazlehurst, and Jesup to Brunswick, gateway to the "Golden Isles."

Laurens County

That wonderful but sadly fading American landmark, the small-town café, is alive and well in Dublin. Ma Hawkins Café, near the Laurens County Courthouse at 124 West Jackson Street, (912) 272–0941, has been a citadel of Southern home cooking since 1931. Now operated by a grandson of the foundress, the cheerful café specializes in Southern-style breakfast—if you've been timid about sampling grits, Ma Hawkins is the place—and lunch and dinner plates highlighted by corn bread, chicken and dumplings, fried chicken, slowly simmered turnip greens and other fresh vegetables, and homemade desserts.

The café's front table is the traditional forum for Dublin's movers and shakers, who congregate throughout the day to jaw about the weather, crops, football, politicals, and the general flow of life. The café is open for breakfast, lunch, and dinner Monday through Saturday. No credit cards are accepted, but it's hard to spend more than $5.

If you'd like to try your own hand at corn bread, using the freshest possible ingredients, head for **Chappell's Mill** (912–272–5128), Highway 441, 13 miles north of Dublin. Built in 1811 and saved from destruction by General William T. Sherman's Union army, the old mill grinds about 15,000 bushels of corn a year into the right stuff for light, golden corn bread. Watch it ground, then buy a two-pound bag for 60¢, five pounds for $1.10. Call before visiting.

Dublin's nineteenth-century Irish heritage is reflected in its annual St. Patrick's Day Festival, a lively round of parades, beauty pageants, arts and crafts, square dancing, softball, and golf tournaments. Along the emerald green lawns of the city's **Bellevue Avenue,** many photogenic Greek Revival and Victorian showplaces parade the year round.

Fish Trap Cut, on the Oconee River off Highway 19 east of Dublin, is believed to be a fish trap built by Indians between 1000 B.C. and A.D. 1050. The historic site includes a large rectangular mound, a smaller round mound, and a canal.

Toombs and Treutlen Counties

The sandy soil of Toombs, Treutlen, and neighboring southeast Georgia counties yields a favorite gourmet delicacy. The **Vidalia Sweet Onion** takes its name from the Toombs County town of

Vidalia. During summer, you can buy 'em by the sackful or carload at roadside stands in and around the town of 10,000.

There's some great Southern eating—onion and otherwise—at the Southern Cafeteria, a fifty-year-old culinary landmark in downtown Vidalia at 102 Jackson Street, (912) 537–9351. Open for breakfast, lunch, and dinner Monday through Saturday and for after-church lunch on Sunday, the cafeteria line glows with golden-fried chicken, catfish, roast beef, pork chops, squash, turnips, corn bread, and, of course, "Vidalia Sweets" done a special way.

Twenty miles north of Vidalia on Highway 29, Sweat's Barbecue is another revered eating tradition in these parts. The barbecue pork, Brunswick stew, and other dishes are especially favored by motorists traveling the services-scant 150 miles of Interstate 16 between Macon and Savannah. Sweat's (912–529–3637) is only 3/10 of a mile south of exit 17 and dishes up the barbecue everyday. The strongest libation is iced tea. You need ask only for "tea," since only cold sufferers, scalawags, and Englishmen drink it hot. And unless you request it unsweetened, it's going to come emphatically presugared. That's a rule to remember whenever you're dining in off-the-beaten-path Georgia.

Evans and Tattnall Counties

Claxton, seat of Evans County, is famous for fruit cakes and rattlesnakes. As you drive into the small town, you're very nearly intoxicated by the sweet aroma of baking fruit cakes. More than 6 million pounds of the holiday treats are produced annually in Claxton's modern bakeries. You can get information on **Fruit Cake Plant Tours** and other area attractions at the Claxton Welcome Center, 4 North Duval Street, Claxton 30417, (912) 739–2281.

If you're here in mid-March, you can take part in the festivities surrounding the annual **Rattlesnake Roundup.** Begun, simply, in 1968 as an effort to reduce the venomous reptile's threat to man and beast, the Roundup has grown into a major happening, with a parade, hundreds of arts and crafts booths, home cooking, and such rattler-related events as awards for the most snakes brought in, the longest, fattest, and so on. A reptile expert "milks" the snakes of their deadly venom, which is used in antivenom serums and other medicines.

In neighboring Tattnall County, Gordonia-Altamaha State Park, P.O. Box 1047, Reidsville 30453, (912) 557–6444, has twenty-five tent and trailer sites with water and electricity, hot showers and rest rooms ($8 a night), a swimming pool, boat dock, and plenty of good fishing places.

Tattnall is also home of a more foreboding institution, the Georgia State Prison, which you can pass by on Highway 178, south of Reidsville.

Dooly County

Barbecue is dear to Georgians' hearts, celebrated in song and story, and exalted at annual festivals such as the **Big Pig Jig** the second weekend of October at the little middle Georgia town of Vienna (*Vie-enna*). Dubbed the "Cadillac of Barbecue Contests" and proclaimed the state of Georgia's official barbecue cooking contest by the state legislature, this is serious business indeed. The winning team takes home prize money, trophies, bragging rights, and the honor of representing Georgia at the annual International Pig Cook-off at Memphis, Tennessee—and just maybe coming back as world champion of the barbecuing arts.

Of course, there's a fun side to all this serious business. Judges sample the secret sauces, which, according to the rules, may include "any non-poisonous substances" and the flavors and textures of ribs, shoulders, and other succulent portions of the porkers. Famished festival-goers also get their chance to savor the entries and take part in a host of other activities. There's always plenty of bluegrass and country music, square dancing and clog dancing, arts and crafts, a 5-kilometer "Hog Jog," and a "Whole Hog Parade," featuring handsome porkers, still not ready for the grill, decked out in all manner of zany costumes.

For information, contact Dooly County Chamber of Commerce, 117 East Union Street, Vienna 31092, (912) 268–4554.

Telfair County

Until July 4, 1986, most motorists passed through the little Telfair County seat of McRae without a second thought. Nowadays, they have something to stop, get out of their cars, and take a picture of. Right in the middle of town, where Highways 341, 441,

280, 23, and 319 come together, there's a replica of the **Statue of Liberty,** a Liberty Bell, and copies of the Declaration of Independence, the Constitution, and other documents. "Miss Liberty" stands thirty-two feet tall—a $1/12$th-scale reproduction of the original in New York Harbor. And she's entirely homemade. Her head is carved from a black gum tree, her torch from cypress, her fiberglass coating created by a McRae boat manufacturer.

Little Ocmulgee State Park, McRae 31055, (912) 868–2832, on Highway 441, 2 miles north of McRae, has fifty-eight tent and trailer sites with water and electricity, hot showers and rest rooms ($8 a night), and ten fully furnished and equipped two-bedroom cottages ($45 a night Thursday through Sunday, $55 Friday and Saturday).

Coffee County

Tobacco, not java, is the economic lifeline of agrarian Coffee County. If you drop by the county seat of Douglas from mid-summer through early fall, you'll see traffic jams of trucks bringing in leaf tobacco from across Southeast Georgia's "Tobacco Belt." The gold leaf is auctioned in the age-old tradition at warehouses around the town and sent off for cigarettes, pipe and chewing tobacco, and snuff. After the hulabaloo of the auction houses, unwind awhile at two tranquil recreation areas.

General Coffee State Park, Nicholls 31554, (912) 384–7082, 6 miles east of Douglas on Highway 32, is an angler's delight. The Seventeen-Mile River (actually fifteen miles long) and a quartet of lakes are rich grounds for catfish, gar, bream, and other freshwater catches. Also in the woodsy 1,480-acre park, you'll find tent and trailer sites, with electricity, water, hot showers, and rest rooms ($8 a night), and pioneer camping with no facilities. If you don't care for fishing, have a picnic or a swim in the large outdoor pool.

The Rocks, 16 miles north of Douglas on Highway 107, is a favorite undeveloped place hereabouts to splash in waterfalls, explore caves, bluffs, woodland trails, and natural camping areas.

Wayne County

If you're a fishing family, you may come close to nirvana in Wayne County. One county removed from the Atlantic Coast,

Wayne includes 60 miles of the Altamaha River, a waterway rich with several varieties of bass, bream, perch, and catfish. **Lake Grace,** on Highway 301 near the Wayne County seat of Jesup, is a local favorite. The 250 acres include plenty of secluded fishing spots, as well as opportunities for boating, swimming, waterskiing, picnics, and camping. Contact the park superintendent at (912) 579–6475.

Pine Lake (912–427–3664), near the small community of Gardi, features a stocked twenty-acre lake tailored for bank fishing. You may also enjoy a swimming pool, shaded picnic areas, and camp sites with electricity, water, and rest rooms.

Jaycee Landing (912–427–7987), on Highway 301 north, has a number of boat ramps in the Altamaha, as well as a general store with food and all your favorite kinds of fishing bait. Camp sites have water, electricity, rest rooms, and showers.

Your camaraderie with local anglers is bound to lead you to some especially rewarding, off-the-beaten path fishing spots!

When you've bagged your limit, enjoy a large sample of Southeast Georgia cooking at Jones' Kitchen, on Main Street in Jesup, (912) 427–4100. The all-you-can-eat daily luncheon spread includes fresh local fish, chicken, meatloaf, vegetables, several kinds of salads, and a peach or apple cobbler for less than you'd pay for lunch at a fast-food outlet.

Jesup, an industrious town of 10,000, has a number of beautifully maintained Victorian homes, which you can drive past with a brochure provided by the Wayne County Chamber of Commerce, P.O. Box 70, Jesup 31545, (912) 427–2028.

Charlton County

Three gateways lead you into the primeval mysteries of the 412,000-acre Okefenokee Swamp National Wildlife Refuge. Suwannee Canal Recreation Area and Stephen C. Foster State Park are in Charlton County, while the Okefenokee Swamp Park is near Waycross, in Ware County.

Administered by the U.S. Fish and Wildlife Service, **Suwannee Canal Recreation Area** is what remains of one man's frustrated efforts to drain the Okefenokee back in the 1880s. He left behind an 11-mile-long waterway that now provides an easy avenue for boaters, fishermen, and sightseers. Along with boat tours—one-hour trips are $8.50 for adults, $4 ages five to eleven—Suwannee Canal has several other visitor amenities.

The Information Center Museum has a fifteen-minute orientation film and exhibits of the swamp's plant and animal life. A boardwalk over the water leads to a forty-foot observation platform. Picnic tables and rest rooms are clustered around the information center. The concession building stocks groceries, cold drinks, insect repellents, and docks for guided boat tours.

A short drive from the concession building and museum, Chesser Island Homestead is the pine and cypress cabin once home to several generations of the Chesser family.

Suwannee Canal Recreation Area, Route 2, Box 336, Folkston 31537, (912) 496–7156, is open daily sunrise to sunset. Drive Highway 121/23 for 8 miles south of Folkston, then turn right (west) at the Okefenokee Refuge sign and continue 3 miles.

Overnight canoeing and two-day to five-day wilderness canoeing and camping adventures are available by advance reservations from the Refuge Manager, Route 2, Box 338, Folkston 31537, (912) 496–3331.

Stephen C. Foster State Park is so far off Georgia's beaten path that to get there from Suwannee Canal you'll have to detour through northeastern Florida. From Suwannee Canal, drive 15 miles south on Highway 23 to St. George, 37 miles west on Highway 94 and Highway 2 in Florida, and back into Georgia at Fargo. From Fargo, go right on Highway 177 and for 18 miles cross a domain of sentinel pines and palmetto thickets, swampy canals, egrets, great blue heron, deer, gators, armadillos, opossum, raccoons, reptiles, and amphibians. Beyond a sign warning that the gates close between sundown and sunup, you arrive at Stephen Foster's compound.

The state park is an eighty-acre island entirely within the Okefenokee National Wildlife Refuge. Rangers conduct boat tours, replete with swamp legends and lore, practical lessons in fauna and flora, and lots of hilarious tall tales. You're bound to see plenty of gators, exotic birds and plants, turtles, and trees. You may also rent boats and canoes and venture forth on you own. There are also a 1/4-mile hiking trail, picnic shelters, a playground, and small museum.

Staying overnight, serenaded by the symphony of the swamp, is an unforgettable experience. Camp sites with electricity, water, hot showers, and rest rooms are $8 a night; two-bedroom cottages, completely furnished with full kitchens and fireplaces, heat, and air-conditioning, are $45 a night Sunday to Thursday, $55

Friday and Saturday. The park's small grocery has minimal supplies, so be sure to stock up before leaving Fargo. You can calm your hunger for a long while with breakfast or lunch at Arti C's Café, on Highway 441, (912) 637–5227. The regular clientele are local loggers, so you'll get a whopping big plateful of hearty, ribsticking chow for a very small price.

Stephen C. Foster State Park, Fargo 31631, (912) 637–5274, is open 7:00 A.M. to 7:00 P.M. from mid-September to the end of February and 6:30 A.M. to 8:30 P.M. from March 1 to mid-September. When the gates are locked at night, only a dire emergency will open them before sunrise. This is done to protect you from roaming critters and the critters from roaming poachers. Also bear in mind that a swamp is full of mosquitoes, other biting pests, and uncomfortable summer heat and humidity. Bring insect repellent and dress comfortably.

In addition to the Folkston route, you may get to the park on Highway 441 to Fargo.

Ware County

Okefenokee Swamp Park, off Highway 1, 8 miles south of Waycross, is the most popular of three entrances to the vast, mysterious "Land of Trembling Earth." Although most of the park is actually outside the boundaries of the 700-square-mile, 412,000-acre Okefenokee National Wildlife Refuge, guided boat tours and cypress boardwalks lead you well into this fascinating world.

The Swamp Park is the most casual visitor-oriented of the three entrances—the others are in neighboring Charlton County—with numerous exhibits, interpretive centers, wildlife shows and other visual displays.

Stop first at the cedar-roofed welcome center adjacent to the paved parking areas. Mounted wildlife exhibits, and the real thing viewed through one-way windows, and a twenty-minute film are an excellent orientation. From there, climb the ninety-foot observation tower, peer into the dark tannic waters from the boardwalk, and see some of the Okefenokee's three dozen varieties of reptiles at the Serpentarium.

Gate admission—$6 adults, $4 ages six to eleven, free under six—includes a 1 1/2-mile guided boat tour and all exhibits and

Okefenokee Swamp Park

shows. A two-hour boat tour ($5 a person) includes an even more extensive look at the hundreds of species of birds, otter, armadillo, black bear, deer, and other critters who inhabit the swamp. You'll also see some of the 15,000 gators as they cruise among the reeds and cypresses like ironclad gunboats. (Back near the welcome center, you'll meet Oscar, the park's fifteen-foot, 900-pound mascot.)

If this two-hour sojourn was too brief, you may arrange with park officials for a guide who'll boat you back into really deep waters, where you may see what song writer Stephen Foster only fantasized: the headwaters of the Suwannee River, which rise in the swamp and flow into Florida.

Okefenokee Swamp Park, Waycross 31501, (912) 283–0583, is open daily in spring and summer 9:00 A.M. to 6:30 P.M., fall and winter 9:00 A.M. to 5:30 P.M.

Nearby **Laura S. Walker State Park,** Waycross 31501, (912) 283–4424, has camp sites with water, electricity, showers, and rest rooms ($8 a night), a swimming pool, playground, fishing, and picnic tables. Chain motels are 10 miles away in Waycross. For some of the finest home cooking hereabouts, head for The Carter House, 514 Mary Street, Waycross, (912) 283–1348.

Huge helpings of down-to-earth food, at down-to-earth prices, are served at daily breakfast, lunch, dinner. For something a bit trendier, try pastas, seafoods, steaks, cocktails at the Duck Pond, 421 Memorial Drive, (912) 285–7009, at lunch and dinner, Monday through Saturday.

Contact Waycross/Ware County Chamber of Commerce, Box 137, Waycross 31502, (912) 283–3742.

Off The Beaten Path in Northwest Georgia

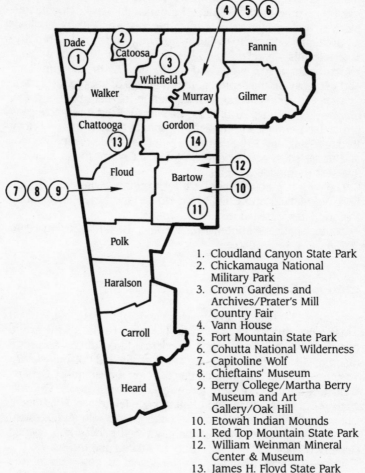

1. Cloudland Canyon State Park
2. Chickamauga National Military Park
3. Crown Gardens and Archives/Prater's Mill Country Fair
4. Vann House
5. Fort Mountain State Park
6. Cohutta National Wilderness
7. Capitoline Wolf
8. Chieftains' Museum
9. Berry College/Martha Berry Museum and Art Gallery/Oak Hill
10. Etowah Indian Mounds
11. Red Top Mountain State Park
12. William Weinman Mineral Center & Museum
13. James H. Floyd State Park
14. New Echota

Northwest Georgia

Dade County

Cloudland Canyon State Park, in far northwest Georgia's remote and rugged Dade County, contains one of the Southeast's most awesome natural sights. The park's namesake and center-piece is a steep canyon cut into the western flank of Lookout Mountain by Sitton Creek Gulch. You may stand by the rim and peer into misty reaches 1,800 feet deep. Better still, lace up your hiking boots, follow woodland trails down to the canyon floor, and get really off the beaten path on 6 miles of backcountry trails.

After you hike, unwind with a swim in the park pool or a few quick sets of tennis. Also in the heavily forested 2,120-acre park are sixteen completely furnished cottages ($45 a night Sunday through Thursday, $55 Friday and Saturday) and seventy-five tent and trailer sites, with electrical and water connections, showers and rest rooms ($8 a night).

The park is a convenient base for exploring Chickamauga National Battlefield and Chief Vann House and New Echota State Historic Sites, detailed in other chapters.

Contact park superintendent, Route 2, Box 150, Rising Fawn 30738, (404) 657–4050.

Catoosa County

In the hellish heat of September 19 and 20, 1863, nearly 130,000 Americans engaged in one of the bloodiest battles of the entire Civil War. When it was over, Confederate forces under the command of General Braxton Bragg had a costly and dubious victory. They had repulsed the outnumbered Union armies under General William Rosecrans but were too weakened to pursue the Federals as they fled to safety around Chattanooga, Tennessee. Subsequent Union victories at Chattanooga's Lookout Mountain and Missionary Ridge and the capture of the city's vital railway hub opened General William T. Sherman's route to Atlanta and the sea.

The 5,500-acre Chickamauga battlefield is now part of the Chattanooga and **Chickamauga National Military Park.** The major sites are adjacent to Highway 27, near Chattanooga and Chickamauga. Stop first at the National Park Service Visitors Center for the audio-visual orientation and the many exhibits. The Fuller Collection of Military Arms has more than 400 weapons from the French and Indian Wars through the present-day conflicts.

Park rangers in Civil War uniforms demonstrate cannon and rifles. The Chattanooga Symphony Orchestra has free outdoor concerts on summer Sunday evenings. Bring a blanket and a picnic supper and join the festivities!

From the visitors center, follow Highway 27 for 3 miles through the park. Battle sites are marked by earthworks, cannon batteries, and farm buildings. Impressive monuments have been placed by states whose sons in blue and gray died here 125 years ago. The park is open all the time. The visitors center is open daily from 8:00 A.M. to 5:45 P.M. Contact the park superintendent, P.O. Box 2128, Ft. Oglethorpe 30742, (404) 866–9241.

Before leaving the area, see Lookout Mountain, Missionary Ridge, and other major parts of the Chattanooga and Chickamauga National Military Park.

Whitfield County

If you've been planning to recarpet your home or cover your pool deck or patio with astroturf, put off that major purchase until you've been to Dalton. Seat of northwest Georgia's green and hilly Whitfield County, industrious Dalton, with a population of 25,000, is the long-reigning "Carpet Capital of the World."

About 66 percent of all the tufted carpeting manufactured in the United States rolls off the giant looms of Dalton's more than seventy-five modern plants. If you're in a buying frame of mind or would just enjoy browsing the latest styles and colors, dozens of outlet stores all around Dalton offer a full range of floor coverings at greatly reduced prices. The Dalton Convention and Visitors Bureau, off Interstate 75's exit 136 at 524 Holiday Drive, (404) 278–7373, can provide you with an up-to-date outlets directory. You can also find out about guided tours of area mills.

Dalton's $5-billion carpeting industry was born around 1900, when a Whitfield County farm girl named Catherine Evans produced a hand-tufted chenille bedspread, copied from a family heirloom, and promptly sold it for the handsome price of $2.50. Enthused by her success, she made more of the brightly colored cotton bedspreads, and these, too, were eagerly snapped up by tourists and local homemakers. Other homebound women began following her lead, and by the early 1920s, tufted bedspreads had grown into a major "cottage industry."

The bedspreads usually featured flowers and other patterns, but the brilliantly plumed male peacock was such a runaway favorite that Highway 41, the major highway leading into Dalton, became popularly known as "Peacock Alley."

In the 1920s, a machine invented in Dalton was able to mass-produce the cotton bedspreads. Another wizard soon realized that by tufting more densely and adding a sturdy backing the same machinery could be adapted to the manufacture of carpeting. Dalton—and households the world over—were never again the same.

The original "cottage craft" of chenille bedspreads is still alive. You can find a practical souvenir with a peacock, Elvis Presley, Jesus Christ, the Confederate battle flag, and other monograms at stores around Dalton and along Highway 41—the original "Peacock Alley"—between Dalton and the Tennessee border. Figure on paying a bit more than $2.50, however!

Some of the early chenille bedspreads are among the exhibits at **Crown Gardens and Archives,** in the original Crown Cotton Mill at 715 Chattanooga Avenue, (404) 278–0217. The museum also has historical displays, a black heritage room, an outdoor spring, and picnic areas.

With its influx of executives and workers from across the nation and several foreign countries, this surprisingly cosmopolitan little city is very active in the fine arts. The Creative Arts Guild, 520 West Waugh Street, (404) 278–0168, is a tastefully contemporary complex with two art galleries and a forum for live theater, dance, and other cultural programs.

Dalton is also a festive city. The Red Carpet Festival, the first weekend of May, celebrates Dalton's famous industry with parades, pageantry, square dancing, bluegrass and gospel music, and plenty of barbecue and other hearty Southern cooking.

On the second weekend of May and October, the **Prater's Mill Country Fair** centers on Benjamin Franklin Prater's circa 1859 grist mill. While the huge mill stones turn out silky cornmeal, 185 artists and craftsmen sell their wares to the tune of bluegrass fiddles, clog dancers, and gospel singers. There are pony rides and other special treats just for the youngsters.

To get the straight scoop on what's happening around town, drop by the Oakwood Café, downtown at 201 West Cuyler Street, (404) 278–2441, at breakfast time and listen in as the local sages cover everything from football to funerals. If you miss them at breakfast, come back at lunch for an update. The Southern-style home cooking is among north Georgia's finest.

When Daltonites are in the mood for a dress-up dinner, they head for The Cellar Restaurant and Lounge, downtown at 101 East Crawford Street, (404) 226–6029. Veal, seafoods, steaks, soups, salads, cocktails, and wines are served at lunch and dinner Monday through Saturday at moderate prices.

Murray County

Vann House was a showplace of nineteenth-century Cherokee accomplishment. At the junction of Highways 52 and 225, 3 miles west of modern-day Chatsworth, the sturdy three-story house, with brick walls two-feet thick, was built in modified Georgian style in 1804 to 1805. Owner James Vann was a half-Cherokee, half-Scot who helped create a Moravian mission for the education of young Cherokees. When he died in 1809, his son Joseph inherited the house and surrounding farmlands. He prospered until 1830, when the state of Georgia confiscated his lands for violating a law forbidding white men to work for Indians.

The Georgia Department of Natural Resources has restored the house and refurnished and redecorated the rooms in early–nineteenth-century style. An intricately carved "floating staircase" is one of Georgia's earliest surviving examples of cantilevered construction. Elsewhere are Bibles, dinnerware, and dining room and bedroom furnishings. Vann House, Chatsworth 30705, (404) 695–2598, is open Tuesday through Saturday 9:00 A.M. to 5:00 P.M., Sunday 2:00 to 5:30 P.M. Adults are $1.50; ages six to twelve, 75¢; under six, free.

On Highway 52, 7 miles east of Chatsworth, **Fort Mountain State Park** is a super-scenic park on a forested, 2,800-foot peak of the Blue Ridge Mountains' Cohutta Range. The park's namesake is a puzzling rock wall, or foundation, that winds nearly 900 feet around the mountainside. Whether it was an ancient Indian fortress, a bastion built by twelfth-century Welsh explorers, or part of some other inscrutable mission is a matter of speculation. The stone observation tower nearby is no mystery. It's a legacy of the Depression Era Civilian Conservation Corps (CCC).

History lessons aside, you may relax in Fort Mountain's lake, hike nature trails, play miniature golf, and set the kids loose on the playground. The 115 camp sites ($8 a night) have water, electricity, hot showers, and rest rooms. Fifteen 2- and 3-bedroom cottages come with kitchen appliances, towels, sheets, and logs for the fireplace at $45 & $55 a night Sunday through Thursday, and $55 and $65 Friday and Saturday. Contact the park superintendent, Chatsworth 30705, (404) 695–2621.

You can really get off the beaten path by plunging into the nearby **Cohutta National Wilderness,** 34,000 acres of mountains, forests, and rivers. Contact the U.S. Forest Service, 401 Old Ellijay Road, Chatsworth 30705, (404) 695–6736.

The best home cooking in these parts is at Edna's Café on Highway 441 in Chatsworth, (404) 695–4951, which puts out superb breakfast and lunch Monday through Friday. Don't miss the coconut and peanut butter pie!

Floyd County

Like its Italian counterpart, Georgia's Rome spreads over seven green hills, in the foothills of the state's northwestern Appalachian Mountains. In the rivers department, the Georgia city of 30,000 has the edge. Instead of one mere Tiber, the Floyd County seat has three: the Etowah and Oostanaula, which join up downtown and form the Coosa. It may not have personages to match the Caesars, but a *dramatis personae* of Cherokee Indian chieftains, Southern aristocrats, cotton traders, Civil War soldiers, and riverboat paddle wheelers have made a rich and colorful cast, all the same. The city got its name quite by chance. In 1834, two traveling salesmen and a cotton planter put their choice of names in a hat. "Rome" was the fortuitous choice, otherwise the city might be known today as Warsaw or Hamburg. A revitalized downtown, focusing on the three rivers, assures Rome of a future as exciting as its past.

Begin your Roman holiday at the Greater Rome Visitor Center

(404–295–5576), a rejuvenated Southern Railway passenger depot, circa 1900, and a retired caboose at 402 Civic Center Drive, off Highway 20 and Highway 27 near downtown. Information is available Monday through Friday 9:00 A.M. to 5:00 P.M.; Saturday 10:00 A.M. to 3:00 P.M.; Sunday noon to 3:00 P.M.

"The Between the Rivers Walking Tour"—it can also be driven, of course—leads you past thirty-eight historic downtown landmarks. If you've been to the Italian Rome, you'll probably recognize the statue in front of City Hall here. The **Capitoline Wolf,** a replica of the Etruscan sculpture on ancient Rome's Capitoline Hill, depicts the city's mythical founders, Romulus and Remus, being nurtured by a she-wolf. It was a 1929 goodwill gift from Benito Mussolini.

The Town Clock, on Clock Tower Hill, is the city's symbol and one of its most beloved landmarks. Built in Waltham, Massachusetts, in 1871, the four 9-foot-diameter clock faces top a handsome brick and cypress water tower.

Myrtle Hill Cemetery, on another of the city's seven hills, is a beautiful tree-shaded sanctuary where Mrs. Woodrow Wilson, 377 Confederate soldiers, and other notables are buried. You're welcome to stroll and admire the panoramic views of Rome's rivers and green hills.

One of downtown's newest "stars" is River Place, an exciting readaptation of a turn-of-the-century brick machinery complex. A three-story, skylighted atrium is flanked by sixteen shops with Georgia crafts, English antiques, apparel, toys, and dolls. Follow your shopping spree with lunch at the attractive Landings at River Place Restaurant, (404) 235–5092. The complex is off Broad Street at the Oostanaula River.

If you don't want to walk or drive on your own, the "Rome Town Trolley," a motorized nineteenth-century-style streetcar, will take you to all the sights, with lots of humor and historical antecdotes.

Chieftains' Museum is Rome's oldest historical landmark. Built as a frontier log cabin in 1794, Chieftains' was the home of Major Ridge, the Cherokee leader who signed a treaty with the U.S. Government that partially contributed to the explusion of the Cherokees from Georgia and the tragic "Trail of Tears." Along with Cherokee history, the museum's artifacts tell the story of Rome as a river town and its role in the antebellum South and the Civil War. An open archaeological dig and a nineteenth-century riverboat are on the grounds. It's at 80 Chatillon Road, off Highway 27, (404) 291–9494. Hours are Tuesday through Friday 11:00 A.M. to 4:00 P.M. Sunday 2:00 to 5:00 P.M.

Rome's most inspiring personality was a determined lady named Martha Berry. Born to privilege in a white-columned Greek Revival mansion, Miss Berry in 1902 founded the Berry Schools to provide educational opportunities to impoverished Appalachian youth. Her original domain of 83 acres has grown to 28,000 acres of handsome buildings, forests, fields, mountains, lakes, and streams. Many students of today's **Berry College** earn their tuition by working on the college's farm, research facilities, and other enterprises.

"The Miracle of the Mountains" is chronicled at the **Martha Berry Museum and Art Gallery,** across from the campus on Highway 27. You'll see a twenty-eight-minute film on her remarkable life and achievements and photos, furniture, and memorabilia. Nearby **Oak Hill** (404–291–1883), built in 1847, is the classic Old South mansion, filled with the Berry Family's antiques and artworks. Around Oak Hill, you're free to wander five acres of tiered formal gardens. The Martha Berry Museum and Oak Hill are open Tuesday through Saturday 10:00 A.M. to 5:00 P.M., and Sunday 1:00 to 5:00 P.M. Admission is adults $1; children 50¢.

You're welcome to drive what's proudly called, "The World's Most Beautiful Campus." Among the Berry College landmarks are the Ford Buildings, a cluster of handsome English Gothic structures and a reflecting pool donated by Henry Ford. Stroll deeper into the campus, bring a picnic, and sit in the cool spray of one of the world's largest overshot waterwheels.

You're also invited to visit the scenic campuses of Shorter College and Darlington Lower School, neighbors on Shorter Avenue west of downtown.

If you'd like to get a little lost in the woods, make an appointment to visit Marshall Forest, on Horseleg Creek Road, off Highway 20, 4 miles west of downtown. The lush 170-acre preserve, administered by the Rome/Floyd County Recreation Authority (404–291–0766), includes 90 acres of fields and 80 acres of forests, where northern red and chestnut oaks mingle with long leaf southern pines. About 300 species of wildflowers and other plants grow on the Flower Glen Trail. The Big Pine Braille Trail offers blind visitors the opportunity to stop at twenty stations describing fifty-three plant species, thirty-one species of trees,

Berry College

and nineteen species of vines and shrubs. Remember to call ahead.

If you've time for only one sit-down meal in Rome, do as the Romans do and head for the Partridge, a citadel of Southern cooking in a one-time movie theater downtown on Broad Street, (404) 291–4048. Grits and biscuits, fried chicken, fish, meatloaf, vegetables, desserts, and other favorites are served at daily breakfast, lunch, and dinner.

Bartow County

Bartow County, along Interstate 75 between Atlanta and Chattanooga, is the site of a fascinating Indian temple mound complex. Here, also, you can visit a small gem of a mineral museum and take a mini-vacation at a state park on a 12,000-acre lake.

Between A.D. 1000 and 1500, the Etowah Indian tribe migrated into the fertile Etowah River Valley, near today's Cartersville, and created a remarkably sophisticated culture. Beans, squash, corn, and fruit that the women cultivated complemented game trapped by the men in surrounding forests and the abundant fish in the Etowah. As part of a vast trading network, the Etowahs made tools, arrowheads, axes, and household implements from Great Lakes copper and Mississippi and Ohio Valley flint. Gulf Coast seashells were fashioned into ceremonial jewelry.

Surrounded by a deep moat and log stockade, a compact city of clay and wooden houses sheltered as many as 4,000 Indians. The heart of the city was half a dozen rectangular earthen mounds. The **Etowah Indian Mounds** were the forum for religious rites conducted by chiefs and priests and the final resting place of these dignitaries.

Stop first at the excellent small museum and reception center, where dioramas and artifacts from the mounds tell the story of this mysteriously vanished tribe. The exhibits are highlighted by a priest's burial chamber and beautifully carved busts of a woman and warrior. A film traces the history of the Etowahs. With a diagrammed map, cross the moat and explore the grass-covered mounds. Ninety-two steps take you up sixty-three feet to the top of Mound "A," from which the priests conducted rituals for the townspeople assembled below in the plaza. Mound "C," one of the smallest, was a principal burial site and the source of most of the artifacts in the museum. Park rangers periodically lead moonlight walks around the site.

About a fifteen-minute drive west of Interstate 75's exit 124, via Highway 113/61, Etowah Mounds State Historic Site, Route 1, Cartersville 30120, (404) 382–2704, is open Tuesday through Saturday 9:00 A.M. to 5:00 P.M. and Sunday 2:00 to 5:30 P.M. Adults are $1.50; ages six to twelve, 75¢; under six, free.

In Cartersville, a congenial town of 10,000, you may want to walk around the downtown shopping area and admire the stately Bartow County Courthouse. Etowah Arts Gallery, 13 Wall Street, (404) 382–8277, sells pottery, paintings, handmade quilts, and other crafts by local artists. Morrell's, a homey, family-run restaurant at 1120 North Tennessee Street, (404) 386–3463, is a popular destination for fried chicken, steaks, children's plates, and Southern breakfast daily.

Red Top Mountain State Park, on exit 123 off Interstate 75 south of Cartersville, is one of the nicest and prettiest in the whole system. A wealth of recreational opportunities, camp sites, and cottages are spread over the wooded hillsides around 12,000-acre Lake Allatoona. During warm weather, you may sun on a sandy beach, swim, and waterski. The rest of the year, bring tennis racquets, fishing gear, picnic supplies, and hiking shoes. Boaters may bring their own or rent houseboats and pontoon boats at the park marina. A small grocery is at the reception center.

Red Top's twenty 2-bedroom cottages ($45 a night Sunday through Thursday, $55 Friday and Saturday) are completely furnished, with fireplaces. The 286 camping sites ($8 a night) have electricity, water, hot showers, and rest rooms. The park office is open daily from 8:00 A.M. to 5:00 P.M. Contact the superintendent, Cartersville 30120, (404) 974–5184.

North of Cartersville, less than a mile from Interstate 75's exit 126, the attractive, well-planned **William Weinman Mineral Center & Museum** is an intriguing stopover for rockhounds and other nature-lovers. Gemstones, minerals, fossils, crystals, arrowheads, geodes, and other specimens are displayed in brightly lighted glass cases. Some are from right here in northwest Georgia's own mineral-mining regions; others are imports from South America, Africa, Australia, Mexico, and the Western United States.

In a simulated limestone cave, with authentic stalactites and stalagmites, you can trace the eons-long formation of caves with easy-to-follow diagrams and explanations. The cave's treasures also include a mastodon's sixty-pound molar and a fossilized box turtle. Other exhibits include a huge array of Indian arrowheads and flint weapons, fluorescent minerals, petrified wood, brilliantly polished geodes, rock crystal, and colorful birthstones. Books, jewelry, and mineral samples are for sale in the gift shop.

The museum, Cartersville 30120, (404) 386–0576, is open Tuesday through Saturday 10:00 A.M. to 4:30 P.M. and Sunday 2:00 to 4:30 P.M. Adults, $1; ages six to twelve, 50¢; five and under, no charge.

Chattooga County

Be sure to bring your fishing gear when you head for **James H. Floyd State Park.** Off Highway 27, 3 miles southeast of the Chattooga County seat of Summerville, the 270-acre park is renowned as one of the state's finest fishing places. A pair of stocked lakes—thirty and thirty-five acres—offer excellent bass fishing opportunities from the banks. Only boats with trolling motors are allowed.

Area fishermen say you can expect to reel in impressive large-mouth bass, as well as big catches of catfish and bream. Youngsters can learn some of the fine arts of fishing during the park's annual fishing rodeo in mid-May. Admission is free, and prizes are awarded for the first, largest, and most fish caught.

Floyd State Park's twenty-five tent and trailer sites ($8 a night) have water and electrical hookups and convenient showers and rest rooms. You'll also find a playground, picnic areas, and hiking trails in the neighboring Chattahoochee National Forest.

Contact park superintendent, Route 1, Summerville 30747, (404) 857–5211.

Gordon County

The Cherokee Indians assimilated themselves into the way of life established by the white settlers, then were ruthlessly crushed out, at **New Echota,** near modern-day Calhoun. In the 1820s, New Echota was laid out as the capital of the Cherokee Nation that included parts of Georgia, the Carolinas, Tennessee, and Ala-

New Echota

bama. Here, the Cherokee legislature formulated laws, enforced by a series of district courts and a supreme court. The Indians wore European-style dress, used American farming methods, and lived in stone and frame houses with the most modern conveniences of the day. The more affluent owned black slaves. The first North American tribe to formulate their own written alphabet, the Cherokees published a bilingual newspaper, circulated as far as Europe.

Gold discovered on Cherokee lands in the late 1820s brought it all to disaster. Supported by President Andrew Jackson, the state of Georgia confiscated all Cherokee lands and in 1838 forced the Indians into exile in what is now Oklahoma. Thousands perished along this "Trail of Tears."

New Echota has been meticulously reconstructed as a state historic site. Stop first to see the orientation slide show and exhibits in the reception center. Then take a self-guided walking tour that includes the Supreme Court Building, the printing presses of the *Cherokee Phoenix* newspaper, and a tavern/general store, and the home of the Reverend Samuel Worcester, a Massachusetts minister who established a mission for the Indians. Park rangers frequently demonstrate arrowhead making and hunting techniques. Books about the Cherokee civilization are on sale at the reception center. In late October, the Cherokee Fall Festival is a weekend of Indian crafts, cooking, and story telling.

New Echota, Route 3, Calhoun 30701, (404) 629–8151, is open Tuesday through Saturday 9:00 A.M. to 5:00 P.M., and Sunday 2:00 to 5:30 P.M. Adults are $1.50; ages six to twelve, 75¢; under six, free.

The restaurant at Shepherd Motel, Highway 53, two blocks off Interstate 75, (404) 629–8644, serves excellent Southern cooking at breakfast, lunch, and dinner daily, with some gourmet surprises.

You may combine New Echota's fascinating lessons with Vann House in neighboring Murray County and the Etowah Indian Mounds, near Cartersville in Bartow County.

Off the Beaten Path in Middle Georgia

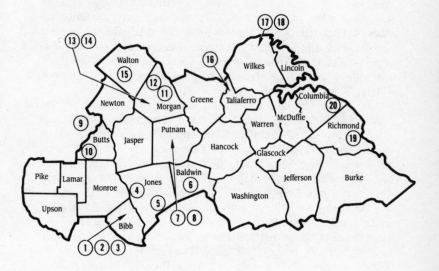

1. Downtown Macon Historic District/Hay House
2. The Harriet Tubman Historical and Cultural Museum
3. Ocmulgee Mounds National Monument
4. Jarrell Plantation/Piedmont National Wildlife Refuge
5. Old Clinton
6. Flannery O'Connor Room/Milledgeville Trolley Tour
7. The Uncle Remus Museum
8. Rock Eagle
9. Indian Springs State Park
10. High Falls State Park
11. Madison-Morgan County Cultural Center
12. Hard Labor Creek State Park
13. Social Circle
14. Burnt Pine Plantation
15. Lake Oconee
16. A. H. Stephens State Historic Park and Confederate Museum
17. Washington Wilkes Historical Museum
18. Kettle Creek Battleground
19. Augusta Trolley Tour/Woodrow Wilson Beauty and Boutique House/Riverwalk Augusta
20. Mistletoe State Park

Middle Georgia

Bibb County

For travelers caught in the relentless grind of interstate traffic, Macon can be a quick and refreshing retreat to a slower, easier era. Only a few minutes from the major highways, **Downtown Macon Historic District** offers a glimpse at beautifully restored Greek Revival and Victorian homes, churches and public buildings on quiet, tree-shaded streets. Three landmark houses are open the year round. Others invite guests during the late March Cherry Blossom Festival.

Make your first stop the Macon-Bibb County Convention and Visitors Bureau, in the Macon Coliseum at Interstate 16 and Coliseum Drive, (912) 743–3401. A free orientation slide show is presented regularly. You may also pick up maps and information for self-guided tours. One of the best ways to catch Macon's Old South–New South spirit is by signing on for Sidney's Old South Historical Tours. Delightful driver-emcee Marty Willett dresses as Macon-born poet Sidney Lanier and laces his historical narrative with humor, anecdotes, and bits of poetry. Don't be startled if he compares his hometown with New Orleans and San Francisco!

With Marty or on your own, the **Hay House** (912–742–8155) will be a highlight. Five years abuilding, the opulent Italian Renaissance palazzo was finished in April 1861 just as Macon and Georgia were marching off to the War Between the States. Behind the stately red brick facade, the twenty-four rooms are a treasure trove of stained glass, statuary, European and American furnishings, silver and crystal, paintings, silk and damask draperies and wall coverings. Long before air-conditioning, a cleverly concealed ventilation system kept the high-ceilinged rooms surprisingly cool even on the most torrid summer days. Located at 934 Georgia Avenue, Hay House is open Tuesday through Saturday 10:30 A.M. to 4:30 P.M. and Sunday 2:00 to 4:00 P.M. Admission for adults is $3; students, $1.50; children, $1.

Just around the corner at 856 Mulberry Street, a white-columned Greek Revival achieved lasting notoriety when a Union shell crashed through the facade and landed in the front hallway. Walk through the Old Cannonball House and adjoining Macon Confederate Museum (912–745–5982) for a look at the stray missile, Civil War photos, artifacts, china, crystal, weapons, uniforms, and such rare treasures as Mrs. Robert E. Lee's rolling pin. It's open Tuesday through Friday 10:30 A.M. to 1:00 P.M. and 2:00 to 5:00 P.M.; Saturday and Sunday 1:30 to 4:30 P.M. Adults are $1; children, 50¢.

Every Georgia schoolchild learns, at least for the moment, Sidney Lanier's romantic poems, "The Marshes of Glynn" and "The Song of the Chattahoochee." Poet, lawyer, linguist, musician, Lanier was born in 1842 in the tidy Victorian cottage at 935 High Street. His desk, furnishings and personal effects are displayed at Lanier Cottage (912) 743–3851) Monday through Friday 9:00 A.M. to 4:00 P.M. Adults are $1; children, 50¢.

The Harriet Tubman Historical and Cultural Museum, downtown at 340 Walnut Street, (912) 743–8544, displays paintings, sculpture, and other creative endeavors by black American, African, and Caribbean artists and craftspeople. The Afro Resources Room has available reference materials and books on black Americans. The museum's shop sells handcrafted jewelry, paintings, posters, recordings, and books. Open Monday through Friday 10:00 A.M. to 5:00 P.M.; Saturday and Sunday 2:00 to 5:00 P.M.

Ocmulgee Mounds National Monument, a short drive from downtown, is a must-see for anyone fascinated by ancient American Indian civilization. A dozen ceremonial and burial mounds, the highest nearly forty-five feet, were built by Mississippian Indians between about A.D. 900 and 1100. They were succeeded at the site by Creeks, who remained here until their forced expulsion to Oklahoma in the 1830s.

Stop first at the National Park Service Visitors Center and see a short film, artifacts unearthed from the mounds, and dioramas on the cultures that flourished here. You may climb steep wooden stairs to the flat top of the forty-five-foot-high Great Temple Mound and to the crest of the surrounding smaller mounds. You may also see them from the comfort of your car. A sound-and-light presentation brings the circular Earthlodge back to life, as tribal elders discuss plans for a war, the effects of a drought, and other important issues. It's at 1207 Emery Highway, (912) 742–0447. Hours are (daily) 9:00 A.M. to 5:00 P.M. Admission is adults $1, twelve and under no charge.

If you have time for only one meal in Macon, make it Len Berg's, downtown in the Post Office Alley, (912) 742–9255. A Macon landmark for many, many years, this comfortable ensemble of small rooms and comfortable booths serves first-class Southern cooking, from fried fish to fried chicken, country fried steak to pork chops, turnip and collard greens, squash casserole and macaroni and cheese, fried okra, biscuits, corn bread, and hot cobblers. Open Monday through Saturday for lunch from 11:00 A.M. to 2:30 P.M. and dinner 5:00 to 10:00 P.M. Prices are very modest, and no credit cards are accepted.

For another taste of Macon, try the plump, juicy hot dogs loaded with chili and other toppings at Nu-Way Wieners, a hometown chain with a downtown outlet at Cherry Street and Cotton Avenue, (912) 743–1368.

To get in the proper antebellum spirit, make reservations at the 1842 Inn, 353 College Street, Macon 31201, (912) 741–1842. The twenty-two guest rooms in the circa 1842 Greek Revival showplace are decorated with antiques, fresh flowers, fireplaces, and all the contemporary comforts. Double rates of about $65 to $90 include continental breakfast.

During the last ten days of March, more than 60,000 Japanese cherry trees set the stage for the city's annual Cherry Blossom Festival highlighted by concerts, home and garden tours, parades, and other activities. You won't be in town very long before proud Maconites tell you that in sheer numbers of blossoming trees, if nothing else, their festival is bigger than Washington, D.C.'s.

Monroe and Jones Counties

Jarrell Plantation is a homespun juxtaposition to the romanticized Old South of Tara and Twelve Oaks, dashing beaux and ladies fair. At the end of a tree-shaded graveled road off Highway 18 between Forsyth and Gray, you enter a world where unrelenting hard work—not flirtation and idle mint juleps—was the rule of society. From the early 1840s, when John Fitz Jarrell built the first dwelling, until 1958 when the last direct heir died, the plantation was worked by three generations of Jarrells. They planted cotton, ran gins and grist mills, and battled boll weevils, depressions, and General William Tecumseh Sherman himself. Nowadays, the dwellings, work buildings, barnyards, and fields are maintained by the Georgia Department of Natural Resources as a living memorial to the state's agricultural heritage.

You'll enter the plantation through the scuppernong arbor,

whose juicy fruit Jarrell women turned into pies and jellies. A flock of guinea fowl, squawking like so many feathered burglar alarms, alerted the family that visitors were approaching. These days, the guinea fowl still sound off, and an assortment of barn-yard animals—a goat, a horse, a brown milk cow, a burro, a couple of sheep—press against the fence for the hay held out by children.

The Visitors Center was the Jarrells' dwelling from 1895 until the 1920s. The solidly built wooden house displays exhibits on the plantation's history and the Jarrell family lineage. With a self-guiding map, take your time strolling around the plantation.

At the 1847 plantation's plain first dwelling, you can visualize the womenfolk sitting in a circle, their hands busily making quilts and clothes, while hearty stews bubbled on the wood-burning stove. At the mill complex down the hill from the house, work-men get the steam engine ready to grind the sugar cane into syrup. In late November, everyone's invited to Sweet Sugar Cane Memories, when the cane is ground and cooked into syrup in big iron kettles, and tea cakes are baked up at the house.

Halloween is another special occasion, especially for children. Storytellers on the porch of the first dwelling recount legends and spooky tales, and youngsters try their hand at games and jack-o'-lantern carving. Over Labor Day weekend, visitors can get a real feel for nineteenth-century farm life by pitching in with the chores. July 4 and Christmas are also celebrated in nineteenth-century rural Georgia fashion.

Jarrell Plantation—Route 1, Box 40, Juliette 31046; (404) 986-5172—is open Tuesday through Saturday 9:00 A.M. to 5:00 P.M. and Sunday 2:00 to 5:00 P.M. Adults are $1.50; children twelve and under, 75¢.

The **Piedmont National Wildlife Refuge,** 10 miles down the graveled road from the plantation, has a visitors center and hiking trails. You can bring your fishing gear and try your luck in the Ocmulgee River.

General William T. Sherman's troops pillaged it; it lost its court-house to a rival town; and over the decades, time has largely passed it by. But **Old Clinton,** off Highway 129, 2 miles south-west of the Jones County seat of Gray, survives as a souvenir of Georgia's early–nineteenth-century frontier. Settled in 1807, Clinton by 1820 was the state's fourth largest town, with fifty-six homes, ten stores, four saloons, law offices, doctors, a cotton gin, and an academy. In 1864 the town became a battleground between Union and Confederate troops, and more than a third of its buildings were reduced to ashes.

Bypassed by progress, the heart of Old Clinton beats on. Fifteen of the earliest structures can be viewed on a walking tour of the historic district. Pick up a brochure at the Old Clinton Historical Society in the McCarthy-Pope House, call Anne Hamilton (912–986–3384) or Martha Madison (912–986–3727). Many of the homes and the Methodist Church reflect the architectural styles of the original New England settlers. A beautiful wrought-iron fence surrounds the Old Clinton Cemetery, where many of those pioneers are buried.

For a taste of authentic Georgia pit barbecue, take a table at Old Clinton Barbecue, on Highway 129 at the edge of the historic district, (912) 986–3225.

Strolling around the very Southern town square in Forsyth, with its granite Johnny Reb defending the Monroe County Courthouse, you'd hardly expect a Parisian-style café to be lurking behind these nineteenth-century storefronts. The Left Banque Restaurant & Market Place (912–994–5505) is a pleasant surprise, indeed, and perhaps a welcome change from barbecue, fried chicken, and traditional Southern cooking. With its Gallic mural, café tables, and lampposts, the dining room does have some of the panache of the Left Bank boulevards.

The luncheon menu is highlighted by superb chicken salad, homemade soups, salads, and sandwiches. Evening fare includes crabmeat-stuffed flounder, chicken Kiev, chicken cordon bleu, veal, and seafood, with housemade cheesecake and other sweets. It's open for lunch and dinner Monday through Saturday at inexpensive to moderate prices. After dinner on Friday and Saturday, the dining tables are pushed back for dancing to jazz and other live bands. The adjacent Market Place shops sell fine jewelry, gifts, antiques, and lingerie.

Baldwin and Putnam Counties

Milledgeville was Georgia's capital city from early after the Revolution until after the War Between the States. Laid out in 1803–1804 on a precise grid of broad streets and public squares, it was the only American city other than Washington, D.C., specifically planned as a capital. In its own way, it was to post-Revolutionary Georgia what Brasilia was to mid–twentieth-century Brazil: a magnet intended to lure settlers away from the comforts of the Atlantic coast.

Statesmen and public officials eased the burdens of the wilderness by building palatial Greek Revival mansions filled with the finest American and European furnishings, books, and art. Halcyon days ended in the fall of 1864 when General William T. Sherman's Union army, marching from Atlanta to Savannah, captured the city.

According to which legend you choose to believe, Milledgeville was spared Sherman's torch because (a) he was met at the outskirts by fellow brothers of the local Masonic lodge, who pleaded for leniency; (b) he didn't want to burn a town he'd chosen as temporary headquarters; (c) he had a local lady friend and did not wish to break her heart.

Whatever the reasons, Milledgeville's peaceable surrender was accomplished when Governor Joseph E. Brown stood in the rotunda of the Governors Mansion and handed his sword to General Sherman. When the "March to the Sea" resumed, the Governors Mansion and everything of nonmilitary importance was left unharmed. The Reconstruction government moved the capital to Atlanta, an action ratified by the state's voters in 1868.

Built in 1835 to 1838 in Palladian design Greek Revival style, the Old Governors Mansion (912–453–4545) has been beautifully restored and refurnished. Guided tours of public rooms rich with original furnishings and fascinating architectural features are conducted Tuesday through Saturday 10:00 A.M. to 5:00 P.M. and Sunday 2:00 to 5:00 P.M. Adults are $1; students, 50¢. It's in the center of the town at 120 South Clark Street.

American literature fans should also visit **The Flannery O'Connor Room** (912–453–5573) in the library of neighboring Georgia College. The late author wrote her two novels (*The Violent Bear It Away* and *Wise Blood*) and short story collections while living here. She died in 1964 and is buried in Memory Hill Cemetery. The Flannery O'Connor Room at her alma mater displays first editions, manuscripts, gifts from admirers, memorabilia and drawings she did as a hobby. It's open Monday through Friday, 8:00 A.M. to 5:00 P.M.

The best way to enjoy the town's heritage is on a two-hour motorized **Milledgeville Trolley Tour,** which covers the major landmarks and includes a visit to the Governors Mansion. Guides weave a wealth of humor and anecdotes into their historical narrative. Tours leave the Milledgeville Tourism and Trade Office, 200 West Hancock Street Milledgeville 31061, Tuesdays and Fridays at 10:00 A.M. Adults are $7, $2.50 ages six to twelve. The tourism office (912–452–4687) also has free maps and information for self-guided walking tours. It's directly across the street from the handsome Baldwin County Courthouse.

First-rate Southern home cooking has made a landmark of Mr. Sirloin (912–452–4812) on Highway 441 north—a no-frills, wonderfully democratic forum that attracts a cross section of clientele, from good ole boys in pickup trucks to social doyennes and shirt-and-tie executives in Cadillacs. Specialties at the cafeteria line include country-fried steak, pork chops, barbecue, fish, chicken, and slowly simmered southern vegetables and corn bread. It's open from 5:15 A.M. to 2:30 P.M. Monday through Saturday.

For dinner Tuesday through Sunday try the crisply fried catfish and hushpuppies, shrimp, and other fresh seafoods at Chobys Landing (912–453–9744), 3090 Highway 441 north and Fisherman's Wharf (912–452–3620), 170 Sinclair Marina Road. Both are on Lake Sinclair, north of town, with docking facilities near the door.

Seekers after celestial barbecue should plan their Milledgeville visit for Friday and Saturday when Hook's Bar-B-Q (912–453–2452), 10 miles east of the city at 713 Sandersville Road/Highway 24, prepares its pit-cooked pork. The meat is slow-cooked over pits behind a humble general store and gas station, and customers are provided tongs with which to extract their own helpings.

Couples and singles who enjoy lodging in historic homes can take home fond memories of the Willis House, 1760 Irwinton Road Milledgeville 31061, (912) 452–2181). The one guest bedroom in the 1830s home has a four-poster bed, private bath, a monumental breakfast, and a chance to meet the friendly ghost-in-residence. Doubles are $100.

After Miledgeville's history lesson, you'll probably be ready for some quiet relaxation. Lake Sinclair, a 15,330-acre, 420-mile shoreline impoundment of the Oconee River, has plenty of stretching room. Marinas, fishing docks, and campgrounds are off U.S. 441 north of Milledgeville. On most days, you'll spot fisherfolk dangling their lines off the highway bridge. Phone 404/526-3646 or 912/452-4687 for camping reservations and fishing information.

Milledgeville's literary lioness was Flannery O'Connor. Eatonton, about 15 miles north on U.S. 441, was the birthplace in 1848 of Joel Chandler Harris, who turned the slave legends he heard as a youngster on a Putnam County plantation into "The Uncle Remus Tales."

The Uncle Remus Museum (404–485–6856), on Highway 441 south of the town of 4,800 has Harris's personal mementoes and illustrations of the tales of the devilish Br'er Rabbit, sly-but-perpetually-outwitted Br'er Fox, dumb ole Br'er Bear, and, of course, the Tar Baby. Also in the log cabin, which was created from two original slave cabins, you'll see first editions, a diorama of an antebellum plantation, and other historical artifacts. The museum is open daily during summer 9:00 A.M. to 5:00 P.M. and closed on Tuesday the rest of the year. Adults are $1; children, 50¢.

As you drive past the Putnam County Courthouse in the center of Eatonton, look for the little likeness of Br'er Rabbit on the lawn, facing Highway 441. Many well-kept antebellum homes are on the shady streets leading off the courthouse square. Putnam County is also the center of Georgia's dairy industry, so you'll also spot several contented herds as you drive out of town.

Rock Eagle, 4 miles north of Eatonton, is a relic of Indian civilizations that flourished here more than 6,000 years ago. A creamy white quartz effigy—about 10 feet high, 103 feet from its head to its tail, 32 feet from wingtip to wingtip—the great bird seems poised for flight. Archaeologists believe Rock Eagle was a focus for Indian tribal rituals. The best views are from an observation tower. It's located in a 4-H Club Center, on Highway 74, off Highway 441.

If you're in the area around Memorial Day, stop by Rock Eagle for the Georgia Folk Festival at the 4-H Club Center. The weekend includes demonstrations of regional handicrafts, square dancing, bluegrass music, and workshops on the ancient Indian cultures of middle Georgia.

The Putnam County Dairy Festival, the first weekend of June, hails this important agri-industry with parades and an arts and crafts fair.

Butts County

A quiet and peaceful recreation place now, **Indian Springs State Park,** near Jackson, has a long, colorful and tragic history. For many centuries, Creeks and other Indians gathered at a sulphur spring whose waters were believed to have magical powers to cure ailments and restore vitality. In the spring in 1825, Creek Indian Chief William McIntosh signed an illegal treaty ceding all tribal lands to the state of Georgia. The fraudulent treaty so enraged the dispossessed Indians that they murdered McIntosh and several of his followers. A valid treaty in 1828 finally ended Creek dominion. The town of Indian Springs was founded, along with what's believed to be the oldest state park anywhere in the United States.

Nowadays, people still flock to the sulfur springs and take home jugs of the strong smelling water. They swear by its ability to restore health and vitality and offer this advice to those who quail at the rottenegg smell: Just let it sit for two to three days, and the aroma will vanish, but not the curative strength of the minerals.

The handsome fieldstone buildings in the park were built during the Great Depression by the Civilian Conservation Corps. Along with the mineral waters, artifacts and historical displays are on view at the Indian Museum. Around a 105-acre lake are a swimming beach, fishing, rental boats, nature trails, and picnic areas. Camp sites with electrical and water hookups are $8 a night. Completely furnished two-bedroom cottages, with log-burning fireplaces, are $45 a night Sunday through Thursday, $55 Friday and Saturday. Contact the park superintendent, Indian Springs 30231, (404) 775–7241.

Fresh Air Bar-B-Que (404–775–3182), on Highway 23 between Jackson and the park, is one of the holy grails of this savory Georgia art form. Except for wooden planking that covered the old sawdust floor a few years ago, and one change of ownership nearly fifty years ago, this rambling, wooden barbecue shack has changed only marginally since it served its first platter in 1929.

The pine board tables have been in place for more than forty years. Pork is slowly cooked over hickory and oak coals right behind the ordering counter. It's sweet and succulent, with a tangy *pièce de résistance* provided by a secret sauce prepared every day by the G. W. "Toots" Caston, patriarch of the family that has operated the place since the early 1940s. Along with barbe-cued pork, the simple menu includes only Brunswick stew, cole slaw, slabs of starchy white bread, soft drinks, and iced tea. It's open Monday through Thursday 7:00 A.M. to 7:30 P.M., Friday and Saturday until 9:30 P.M., and on Sunday until 8:30. During the summer, it usually remains open a half hour to an hour later.

If you're not a barbecue fan, you might try the Southern home cooking at the Mason Jar (404–775–6525), a small café on Jack-son's courthouse square, for breakfast and lunch.

High Falls State Park, off Highway 36, about 12 miles south of Indian Springs, is another rustic off-the-beaten path retreat. The centerpiece is a series of scenic white-water cataracts of the Towaliga River rushing over mossy rocks. According to legend, Creek Indians "cured" their victims' scalps around the Towaliga—hence the name, which means "roasted scalp."

Two hiking trails offer views of the falls, the river, and adjacent woodlands. You can wade into the river but be extremely careful of the slick, mossy rocks. Also in the 995-acre park, you'll find a 650-acre lake for fishing and boating, a swimming pool, and 142 tent and trailer sites, with water and electrical hookups for $8 a night. Contact the park superintendent, Route 5, Box 108, Jackson 30233, (912) 994–5080.

After a vigorous day in the park, head for dinner at the Falls View Restaurant (912–994–6050), across the highway. The rustic log cabin draws droves of locals with its inexpensive menu of fried catfish and hushpuppies, broiled and fried flounder, shrimp, oysters, chicken, steak, and salad bar. It's open Monday through Thursday 4:30 to 9:00 P.M., Friday and Saturday until 9:30. Closed Sunday.

Morgan and Walton Counties

Morgan County, between Augusta and Atlanta, claims Madi-son, one of Georgia's prettiest antebellum towns. Before leaving, you can relax at a state park with an eighteen-hole golf course, fish and swim at a 19,000-acre lake, and hunt quail on a private preserve.

Strolling the tree-shaded streets and picturesque town square, admiring Madison's treasury of glorious antebellum architecture, we should say "thank you" to a United States senator who put himself between the town and General William T. Sherman's torch. In late 1864, Atlanta in ruins 60 miles away and the cruel "March to the Sea" in full stride, Sherman's Union army approached Madison's outskirts. They were met by former Senator Joshua Hill, a foe of secession who'd been acquainted with Sherman in Washington. He peacefully surrendered the town, which was miraculously spared war's ravages.

You should stop first at the **Madison-Morgan County Cultural Center,** 434 South Main Street, Madison 30650, (404) 342–4743. The Romanesque-style red brick schoolhouse, circa 1895, is now the hub for regional arts, theater performances, and the source of walking-tour maps of the fetching little town of 3,000. The former school rooms now show pottery, weaving, paintings by Georgia artists and traveling exhibitions, nineteenth-century furniture, farm implements, clothing, Civil War artifacts. You may also see a log cabin from the early 1800s and an 1890s school room, complete with pot-bellied stove and hickory switch. The Center's August theater festival features everything from Shakespeare to Tennessee Williams. The Center is open Monday through Friday 10:00 A.M. to 4:30 P.M. and Saturday and Sunday 2:00 to 5:00 P.M. Admission is $2 adults; students, $1; no charge on Wednesday.

With a self-guided tour map, walk through the Madison National Historic District and admire more than three-dozen gorgeous Greek Revival, Neoclassical, Victorian, Federal, and Romanesque homes, many of them graced by gardens and stately trees. A number of these old beauties are open to the public during Madison's May and December festivals.

Madison's town square is one of Georgia's most delightful, the Morgan County Courthouse one of the grandest of the 159. Several antique and handicraft stores will draw your attention as you stroll around the square. When hunger strikes, head for the cafeteria line at Ye Old Colonial (404–342–2211), a unique dining landmark on the square. Once upon a time the building was a bank, which accounts for the high ceilings, tiled floors, and a small dining room in the one-time vault. These days, you can cash in on excellent fried chicken, barbecue, fish, Southern-style vegetables, and hearty breakfasts with biscuits and buttery grits. Service is continuous from breakfast through lunch and dinner Monday through Saturday.

Hard Labor Creek State Park, 12 miles west of Madison,

near the small community of Rutledge, is a nice place to relax for a day, or several days. The recreational possibilities include a very good eighteen-hole golf course and a lake for swimming, boating, and fishing. Plenty of picnic tables are spread among the pines, and there's a playground for the youngsters. If you're planning to play the 6,682-yard, par-72 course, bring your own clubs. You may rent an electric cart in the clubhouse, which has showers and a snack bar. The park's fifty camp sites ($8 a night) have water, electricity, rest rooms, and showers; twenty 2-bedroom cottages ($45 a night Sunday through Thursday, $55 Friday and Saturday) are completely furnished, including towels, sheets, and kitchen utensils. The park office is open daily 8:00 A.M. to 5:00 P.M. Contact the superintendent, Rutledge 30663, (404) 557–2863

The little Walton County town of **Social Circle,** about 8 miles west of Hard Labor Creek on Highway 11, is a delightful place to stroll and browse. The nineteenth-century storefronts have been brightly repainted, and three are antique shops. The wooden shelves in the old mercantile store are stacked to the ceiling with canned goods, overalls, farm products, and household necessities. The town allegedly got its name when a stranger happened onto a cluster of idling locals and found them so friendly he proclaimed, "Why, this is sure some social circle."

You can continue north on Highway 11 to the Walton County seat of Monroe, a quiet small town with tree-shaded courthouse dating to 1883. The inscription on the Confederate monument reads:

> On Fame's Eternal Camping Ground,
> Their silent tents are spread,
> And glory guards with solemn round,
> The bivouac of the dead.

As you drive between Social Circle and Monroe on warm weekends, look for a wealth of yard sales; they often include a barbecue.

Burnt Pine Plantation, a 10,000-acre spread of fields, woodlands, and hedgerows near Madison, is a private preserve dedicated to the sport of quail and dove hunting. Guests are furnished with guides and dogs. Accommodations and meals are at a comfortable lodge and adjacent, fully furnished cottages. Contact Burnt Pine Plantation, 2250 Newmarket Parkway, Marietta 30067, (404) 953–0326.

Lake Oconee, (404–526–3646), a mammoth Georgia Power

Company impoundment of the Oconee River, is a major destination for outdoor recreation. The 19,000-acre lake, with a 375-mile shoreline, has numerous marinas, camp sites, picnicking areas, and swimming beaches. The Georgia Power Company office at the lake (404–485–8704) can supply further information about recreational facilities. Like Morgan County's other main attractions, the lake is easily accessible from Interstate 20.

Taliaferro County

Two miles off Interstate 20's exit 55, drowsy little Crawfordville is small-town America of a long-gone yesteryear. Guarded by a granite Johnny Reb, the red brick Taliaferro ("Tolliver" in the English fashion) County Courthouse presides over a quiet square, where old gentlemen sit and gossip under sidewalk arcades. Tranquil as it is, Crawfordville has significant historic and culinary treasures.

In her cheery café across from the courthouse, Mrs. Annie Lou Bonner has created state-of-the-art sweet potato pie and other stars of the Southern galaxy since 1926 at Mrs. Bonner's Café (404–456–2347). Deep burnt-orange in hue, fragrant with ginger, cinnamon, and nutmeg, the creamy sweet potato filling rests atop a thin, flaky crust that Mrs. Bonner prepares from scratch every morning. Before the pie have a plate of her fried chicken, baked ham, barbecue, or pork chops, with fresh vegetables and corn bread and a large glass of sweetened iced tea, and for less than $5, you've taken a long look into the Southern soul. She's on hand from early morning to late at night Monday through Saturday.

Two blocks from Mrs. Bonner's Café, **A. H. Stephens State Historic Park** includes the homes and gravesite of Alexander Hamilton Stephens, governor of Georgia and vice-president of the Confederacy. Liberty Hall, the two-story frame house Stephens built around 1830, is filled with his furnishings, personal effects, and the wheelchairs to which he was bound much of his life.

The adjoining **Confederate Museum** (404–456–2602) is highlighted by a bronze statue of Stephens by Gutzon Borglum, sculptor of the U.S. presidents on Mount Rushmore, South Dakota. This fine collection of memorabilia also includes dioramas of soldiers in the heat of battle and the quiet of the campfire; rifles and shot; field gear; battle flags; and touching personal

A.H. Stephens State Historic Park

belongings—Bibles, prayer books, and bloodstained photos of wives and sweethearts.

As in all wars, Civil War soldiers used sharp-edged humor to help blunt the insidious enemies of fear and homesickness. "In this army," a Confederate foot soldier wrote, "one hole in the seat of the breeches indicates a captain, two holes is for a lieutenant, and the seat of the pants all out is for us privates." Liberty Hall and the Confederate Museum are open Tuesday through Saturday 9:00 A.M. to 5:00 P.M. and Sunday 2:00 to 5:30 P.M. Adults are $1.50; ages five to twelve, 75¢; under age five, no charge.

After your history lesson, relax at the park's recreation area. A quarter mile from Liberty Hall, you'll find a swimming pool, two fishing lakes, picnic shelters, and thirty-six tent and trailer sites, with water and electrical hookups, showers, and rest rooms ($8 a night).

Aside from Mrs. Bonner's, Crawfordville has another culinary landmark. Heavy's Barbecue, across Interstate 20 from the town, serves hearty Georgia-style barbecue in a museumlike dining room. It's open only Friday, Saturday, and Sunday.

Wilkes County

Incorporated in 1780, the picture book little town of Washington was the first American community named in honor of the father of our country. Skirted by General William T. Sherman's rampaging "March to the Sea," treated kindly by progress and time, the town of about 5,000 is like a living Williamsburg. More than thirty Greek Revival homes, churches, and public buildings predate 1850. Most of them are still well-maintained residences. Three antebellum landmarks are open to visitors the year round.

The Robert Toombs House State Historic Site, 216 East Robert Toombs Avenue, (404) 678–2226, was the home of Georgia's "Unreconstructed Rebel," U.S. senator, and Confederate secretary of state. At odds with the Confederacy—he was resentful of Jefferson Davis's presidency—as well as the Union, he fled to the Caribbean and Europe after the war. Returning in 1880, he scorned political pardon. "I am not loyal to the government of the United States," he declared, "and do not wish to be suspected of loyalty." The guided tours of his Greek Revival house include a documentary film, anecdotes, historical exhibits, and several rooms with period furnishings. Open Tuesday through Saturday 9:00 A.M. to 5:00 P.M. and Sunday 2:00 to 5:30 P.M. Adults are $1; children five to twelve, 50¢; under age five no charge.

The **Washington-Wilkes Historical Museum,** 308 East Robert Toombs Avenue, (404) 678–2105, houses an outstanding collection of Civil War artifacts including Jefferson Davis's camp chest (given to him by English sympathizers), weapons, uniforms, signed documents, photographs, and furnishings. The main floor of the circa 1835–1836 two-story frame house is furnished as a typical nineteenth-century double parlor, dining room, and bedroom. The ground floor has been restored as a period kitchen. The grounds are noted for beautiful landscaping and one of Georgia's largest camellia gardens. Hours are Tuesday through Saturday 10:00 A.M. to 5:00 P.M. and Sunday 2:00 to 5:00 P.M. Adult admission is $1; children, 50¢.

Callaway Plantation, 5 miles west of Washington on Highway 78, (404) 678–7060, is a living heritage museum, rich in lessons about Southern antebellum life. Three restored homes and the adjoining farm are like a walk back in time. The red brick, white-columned manor house was the heart of a 3,000-acre cotton plantation. Rooms are furnished with period antiques and many unique architectural features. The outbuildings include a hewn log cabin, circa 1785, with early domestic and agricultural tools and primitive furniture; a smokehouse, barn, pigeon house, and cemetery. Surrounding fields are planted with cotton, corn, cane, and vegetables, just as they were in the mid-nineteenth century. The plantation has been owned by the same family since the late eighteenth century, and it's open Tuesday through Sunday 10:00 A.M. to 5:00 P.M. Adults are $1; children, 50¢.

Washington also figured in the Revolutionary War. A marker at **Kettle Creek Battleground,** 8 miles south of town on Highway 44, commemorates the patriots' 1779 rout of the British and the Redcoats' subsequent withdrawal from this area of Georgia. Picnic tables are at the site.

When hunger overwhelms your hunt through history, head for Another Thyme (404–678–1672), an attractive café in the lobby of the Victorian Fitzpatrick Hotel on the courthouse square. Fare includes sandwiches, soups, salads, plate lunches, and home-made desserts Monday through Friday. The Crock Pot, 103 Lexington Avenue, (404) 678–4540, serves soups, salads, sandwiches, beer, and wine Monday through Saturday.

You may sleep in the bower of history at four moderately priced bed and breakfasts: Water Oak Cottage, 211 South Jefferson Street, (404) 678–3548 or 678–3605; Anderson's Guest Cottage, 401 South Alexander Street, (404) 678–7538; Liberty Street Inn, 108 W. Liberty Street, (404) 678–3107; and the Olmsteads, Pembroke Drive, (404) 678–1050.

Richmond County

Augusta, a city of 50,000 with 250,000 in the metropolitan area, traces its heritage back to 1736, when General James Edward Oglethorpe, father of the Georgia Crown Colony, laid it out as the state's second city, after Savannah. Fought for during the Revolutionary War, skirted by General William T. Sherman's "March to the Sea," Augusta has mild winters and a genteel Old Southern life-style that caught the attention of post–Civil War Northern aristocrats, who found the right formula for golf—a pastime that symbolizes this city to sportsmen around the world.

The **Augusta Trolley Tour,** a modern motorized tram with a nineteenth-century appearance, is one of the easiest, most fun, and interesting ways of seeing a cross section of the city's historic landmarks, museums, and restored Victorian neighborhoods. Tours depart from the Sacred Heart Cultural Center downtown, on Thursdays and Saturdays at 10:00 A.M., make seven stops, and continue until 5:00 P.M., returning to each stop every hour. You may ride the trolley for an hour and see the sights or disembark at any stop and get back on when it returns.

All-day tickets are $1.50 for adults and 75¢ for students and senior citizens. Children under age six ride free. Tickets may be purchased at the Sacred Heart Gift Shop, (404) 826–4701. For information, call the Augusta Public Transit Infoline: (404) 722–2034.

Whether on the trolley or on your own, you'll find numerous places of interest around the downtown area.

Sacred Heart Cultural Center, 1301 Greene Street, (404) 826–4700, is a heartening and very spectacular example of a cherished piece of architectural heritage, down on its luck, given a new lease on life. Consecrated in 1901, the red brick, twin-spired Romanesque Catholic church summed up the highest skills of European artists. Jewel-like tones of German stained-glass windows played against the creamy white Italian marble of columns, stations of the cross, and the ornate high altar. In the early 1970s, with much of its congregation now in the suburbs, Sacred Heart's doors were closed, the church deconsecrated and left to the mercy of the elements and vandals.

The church would probably have kept a date with the wrecking ball if an "angel" in the form of an affluent and civic-minded corporate executive hadn't come to the rescue. Following an extensive renovation, Sacred Heart Cultural Center is now the scene of banquets, wedding receptions, fashion shows, chamber concerts, and numerous other functions. A gift shop on the lower floor sells works by local artists and authors. You may take a self-guided tour of the sanctuary Monday, Tuesday, Wednesday, and Friday between 8:30 A.M. and 5:30 P.M.; donations are accepted. Guided tours are led Thursday and Saturday 10:00 A.M. to 4:00 P.M. and Sunday 1:00 to 4:00 P.M. Adults are $2; senior citizens and students, $1.

Ezekiel Harris House, 1840 Broad Street, (404) 733–6768, is Augusta's second-oldest structure. In 1797 Harris came to the area from South Carolina with plans to build a town to rival Augusta as a tobacco market. On a hill overlooking Augusta, the house is an outstanding example of post-Revolutionary architecture. The gambrel roof and vaulted hallway are reminiscent of New England. Tiered piazzas are supported by artistically beveled wooden posts. Rooms are furnished with period antiques. It's open Monday through Friday 9:00 A.M. to 4:30 P.M. Adults are $2; students, 50¢.

Meadow Garden, Independence Drive near the intersection of Walton Way and 13th Street, (404) 724–4174, was the home of George Walton, one of Georgia's signers of the Declaration of Independence. Built around 1791, it's the city's oldest documented structure and has been restored and refurnished by the Georgia Society, Daughters of the American Revolution. Hours are Monday through Friday 9:00 A.M. to 4:00 P.M., Saturday 10:00 A.M. to 4:00 P.M., Sunday 1:00 to 4:00 P.M. Admission for adults is $2 ($1 with trolley ticket) and 50¢ for children.

If you enjoy flea markets and antique stores, you'll have a field day at the Augusta-Richmond County Museum, 540 Telfair Street, (404) 722–8454. The castlelike Romanesque building, dating back to 1802, is really Augusta's municipal "attic." The maze of hallways and galleries is crammed with Mexican pottery, Peruvian folkloric costumes, Civil War weapons and uniforms, World War I gas masks, stuffed birds and butterflies, a DC-3 aircraft, a circa 1915 steam locomotive, Audubon bird and wildlife prints, vintage photos, African masks, Revolutionary War dioramas, Victorian firemen's gear, and much, much more. It's open Tuesday through Saturday 10:00 A.M. to 5:00 P.M. and Sunday 2:00 to 5:00 P.M. Admission for adults is $2; ages six to eighteen and senior citizens, $1.

The museum is in the heart of the Telfair Historic District, also known as Olde Town, where numerous Victorian mansions are being given new life as inns, apartments, shops, and offices.

Gertrude Herbert Institute of Art, 506 Telfair Street, (404) 722–5495, is an architecturally outstanding early–nineteenth-century residence that showcases regional and Southeastern contemporary art. Built in 1818 by Augusta Mayor Nicholas Ware, the elliptical three-story staircase, Adam-style mantels, and other rich ornamentation earned it the name, "Ware's Folly." Hours are Tuesday through Friday 10:00 A.M. to 5:00 P.M. and Sunday 1:00 to 4:00 P.M. Admission fees are adults, $1; children, 50¢.

You can have your hair styled in President Woodrow Wilson's boyhood home. The two-story brick house, built around 1860, was the parsonage for the First Presbyterian Church. The future president lived here from age two to fourteen, while his father was pastor. It's now the **Woodrow Wilson Beauty and Boutique House,** a center of the cosmetological arts, as well as a gift shop and florist. The owner will be happy to show you through the historic rooms, which contain memories of our World War I president. It's downtown at 419 7th Street at Telfair Street, (404) 722-4556.

For many years, Augusta almost forgot that the Savannah River ran by its doorstep. All that is changing rapidly as **Riverwalk Augusta** becomes a new center of downtown activity. The main entrance to Riverwalk is at 8th and Reynolds streets, a block off Broad Street. The top of the old river levee has been turned into an inviting brick esplanade with seating clusters overlooking the river, historical displays, and playground and picnic areas. Major hotels, shops, and dining are also in the works.

For dining in the downtown area, you've a choice of something old, something new. The Town Tavern, 15 7th Street at the Riverwalk, (404) 724–2461, recently celebrated its fiftieth anniversary. The American menu includes seafoods, steaks, salads, and full Southern breakfast in an attractive Early American motif. It's open for breakfast, lunch, and dinner Monday through Saturday. Credit cards are accepted, and prices are moderate.

Palmer's Seafood House, 201 Riverfront Drive, (404) 722–0011, is a newcomer from Savannah, with an outdoor terrace overlooking the river. Lunch and dinner are served Monday through Saturday. Credit cards are accepted, prices moderate.

If you're into antiquing, head for the 1200 block of Broad Street, where you'll find an extensive cluster of shops and flea markets.

Kids and kids at heart shouldn't miss Fat Man's Forest (404–722–0796). A rambling array of added-on buildings at 1545 Laney-Walker Boulevard, Fat Man's is locally renowned for its holiday paraphernalia. At Halloween, people come from miles around to rent costumes, purchase pumpkins and made-to-order jack-o'-lanterns, and send their youngsters through the haunted house. At Christmas, the kids ride a festive train while grownups browse for trees, gifts, and decorations. Whatever the season, it's a fun place to wander and marvel at the Fat Man's ingenuity.

For golfers around the globe, Augusta is Christmas, the World Series, the rainbow's end. In late March and early April, fortunate faithful congregate along the dogwood-and azalea-rimmed fairways of storied Augusta National Golf Club to hail the game's elite as they pursue the Green Jacket, symbolic of the Masters Tournament championship. Unless you know a player or a club member, tickets to the championship rounds will be impossible to find. But don't despair. You can see all the greats up close—even take their pictures—during the practice rounds preceding the tournament. You'll have to get in line early at Augusta National's ticket booths, for $15 tickets Monday and Tuesday, $20 for the par-3 tourney on Wednesday.

If you'd like to play, the new Jones Creek Course, an eighteen-hole public layout at 4101 Hammonds Ferry Road, (404) 860–4228, is considered the "poor man's" Augusta National. Designed by renowned golf architect Rees Jones, it has an excellent practice facility and professional instructors. Rental clubs and carts are available.

Ever wondered how a daily newspaper is put together? *The Augusta Chronicle-Herald*'s free tour has all the answers. The one-hour guided tour takes you through the busy newsrooms and feature departments, into the printing plant, where type is set, pages assembled and published on high-speed presses at Broad Street, downtown, (404) 724–0851.

The Telfair Inn, 326 Greene Street, (404) 724–3315, is a beautiful example of practical restoration. Seventeen Victorian residences were rejuvenated, redecorated, and refurnished in nineteenth-century fashion, with wood-burning fireplaces and all the modern comforts, and turned into a lovely downtown inn. Rates of $45 to $65 single, $55 to $75 double, include a colossal Southern breakfast.

The Perrin Guest House Inn, near Augusta National at 208 Lafayette Drive, (404) 736–3737, has ten guest rooms and an elegant restaurant with an extensive wine list. Doubles range from $65 to $115.

Bass fishermen and those seeking more off-the-beaten-path relaxation should look into a mini-vacation at **Mistletoe State Park.** About 35 miles north of Augusta, on 76,000-acre Clark Hill Reservoir, this very tranquil park reputedly commands some of America's finest bass fishing waters. You may also swim and boat in the lake, hike 5 miles of woodland trails, and ride rental bikes around the 1,920 acres. Two-bedroom furnished cottages are $45 a night Sunday through Thursday, $55 Friday and Saturday; camping sites are $8, with water, electricity, showers, and rest rooms. Contact the park superintendent, Appling 30502, (404) 541–0321.

Off the Beaten Path in Coastal Georgia

1. Savannah National Historic District/Emma's
2. Fort Jackson/Oatland Island Education Center
3. Fort Pulaski National Monument
4. Tybee Island Museum and Lighthouse
5. Skidaway Island State Park/Wormsloe State Historic Site
6. Fort McAllister State Historic Park
7. Midway Church/Sunbury
8. Fort King George State Historic Site
9. Sapelo Island Tours
10. Hofwyl-Broadfield Rice Plantation
11. Old Town Preservation Association/Mary Miller Doll Museum
12. Jekyll Island Club Historic District
13. Fort Frederica National Monument/Christ Church/St. Simons Lighthouse
14. Cumberland Island National Seashore
15. Crooked River State Park

Coastal Georgia

Chatham County

Founded in 1733 as the seat of England's Georgia Crown Colony, Savannah is one of America's truly special cities. The founding father, General James Edward Oglethorpe, planned the city on a precise grid of broad, straight thoroughfares intersecting public squares at regular intervals. Initially conceived as mustering places for militia, the squares eventually became public gardens, embellished with fountains, trees, flowers, and monuments to Revolutionary heroes. In the prosperous years before the Civil War, wealthy cotton brokers and shipbuilders flanked the squares with stately residences in English Regency, Federal, Georgian, Neo-Gothic, and other styles.

A post–Civil War collapse of the cotton market inadvertently saved much of this noble architecture from destruction. Since the mid-1950s, an ongoing campaign has restored nearly 2,000 historic residences, churches, and pubic buildings in the 2.2-square mile **Savannah National Historic District,** the largest in the nation.

One of the simple pleasures of visiting Savannah is sitting in the squares and leisurely admiring the rich ornamental details of the monuments and eighteenth- and nineteenth-century buildings. No matter how many times you've been here, no matter how many times you've looked, you'll always see something that previously eluded your gaze. This intriguing factor makes even the most beaten track into an off-the-beaten-path adventure.

With its compact dimensions and so much to see, Savannah is a walker's delight, especially in spring when millions of azaleas, dogwoods, and other flowering plants turn the whole city into a pastel-shaded movie set. You can also rent bikes or ride in a horse-drawn carriage. Orient yourself to the city by stopping first at the Savannah Visitors Center, in the red brick, 1860s Central of Georgia Railroad Depot, at 301 West Broad Street, downtown, (912) 944–0456. Watch a free orientation slide show and pick up brochures, maps, and information about points of interest.

Numerous guided tours in air-conditioned vans leave from the Visitors Center. One of the best ways to see the city from an insider's perspective is to take a walking tour with Square Routes (912–232–6866), a small, personalized company that specializes in off-the-beaten-path looks at private gardens and mansions, hidden-away bookshops and antique stores, and other places you'd never find on your own. Guides spice their walks with ghost stories, gossip, and scandals past and present.

If you are on your own, one of the best places to start is the riverfront. On Bay Street, standing on bluffs above the Savannah River, a row of red brick buildings known as Factors Walk was the hub of Savannah's pre–Civil War cotton economy. The cotton itself was stored in brick warehouses below the offices as it awaited shipment to mills in England and New England. As a major element of the city's rejuvenation, the old brick warehouses have been remodeled as seafood restaurants, taverns, shops, and art galleries, and flanked by a broad esplanade called Riverfront Plaza, also known as River Street. Benches are excellent places to sit and watch the colossal cargo ships heading for the docks and industries up the Savannah River or to the open Atlantic, 20 miles downriver.

The Ships of the Sea Museum, 503 River Street/Riverfront Plaza, (912) 232–1511, is a natural complement to the city's maritime heritage. Three floors shine with ornamental figureheads, scrimshaw artistry, a chandler's shop, ships-in-bottles, sailing ship models, and other artifacts. It's open daily 10:00 A.M. to 5:00 P.M. Adults are $2; ages seven to twelve, 75¢.

The museum's top floor is on Bay Street, a convenient starting point for walking tours of the downtown squares and important landmarks. The most popular walking route takes you from the front of Savannah's ornate City Hall—the dome was recently regilded—south on Bull Street to Forsyth Park. Along the way, you'll cross Johnson, Wright, Chippewa, Madison, and Monterey squares. Each has a monument to a bygone hero and landmarks that played important parts in the city's history.

Revolutionary War hero General Nathanael Greene is buried beneath the granite shaft in Johnson Square. Wright Square honors the founder of the Central of Georgia Railroad.

At Bull Street and Oglethorpe Avenue, Girl Scouts and students of American history should pause at the Juliette Gordon Low Girl Scout National Center (912–233–4501). Built in the early-nineteenth century by noted English architect William Jay, the dignified English Regency mansion was the 1860 birthplace of "Daisy" Low, founder of the Girl Scouts of America. Daisy's paintings and sculpture, personal effects, and GSA mementoes are displayed in the high-ceilinged rooms. It's open Monday through Saturday 10:00 A.M. to 4:00 P.M. and Sunday 12:30 to 4:30 P.M. Adults are $2.50; students, $1.75; under age six, no charge.

A bronze statue of General Oglethorpe, by Daniel Chester French, highlights Chippewa Square. Madison Square's centerpiece honors Sergeant William Jasper, killed in the Revolutionary battle for the city in 1779. From the Green-Meldrim House General William T. Sherman telegraphed President Lincoln a Christmas gift of the city, which had peacefully surrendered on December 14, 1864. It's now the parish house for St. John's Episcopal Church.

The marble column in Monterey Square honors Casimir Pulaski, a Polish count who died in the 1779 siege. Congregation Mickve Israel (912–233–1547), on the east side of Monterey Square, traces its heritage back to July 11, 1733, only five months after General Oglethorpe established the colony. Some descendants of the original Jewish settlers still worship at the handsome Gothic synagogue, completed in 1878. If you come to the side door Monday through Friday between 10:00 A.M. and noon, a member of the congregation will show you the sanctuary, tell the history of the congregation, and let you browse through a small museum with a deerskin Torah, documents, and ceremonial pieces that date back to the original settlers.

East and west of Bull Street, Whitefield, Lafayette, and Troup Squares are surrounded by restored residences in a variety of architectural styles. The King-Tisdell Cottage at 514 East Huntingdon Street (912–234–8000) is headquarters for "Negro Heritage Trail Tours," which include landmarks of the city's black history, going back to the arrival of the first slaves. Built in 1896, the cottage is a museum of coastal Georgia black history and noteworthy for its Victorian furnishings and "gingerbread" ornamentation. Hours are Monday through Friday 10:00 A.M. to 4:30 P.M. and weekends 1:00 to 4:00 P.M. Admission for adults is $1.50; children, 75¢.

The Davenport House on Columbia Square played a vital role in Savannah's restoration movement. Built between 1815 and 1820 and considered one of America's most perfect Georgian mansions, the house was threatened in the 1950s with demolition to make room for a funeral home parking lot. The Historic Savannah Foundation saved the Davenport and has since led the effort to save hundreds of other historic structures. Now a museum, the restored Davenport (912–236–8097) gleams with Chippendale and Sheraton furnishings, woodwork, and plaster crown mouldings. Visitors are welcome Monday to Saturday 10:00 A.M. to 4:30 P.M. and Sunday 1:30 to 4:30 P.M. Admission fees are adults $2.50, children $1.25. (Incidentally, the funeral home has long since closed and is up for sale.)

The Marquis de Lafayette slept at the Owens-Thomas House (912–233–9743) on nearby Oglethorpe Square during an 1825 farewell tour of the young nation he'd helped so significantly to establish. Guided tours point out the side balcony from which he addressed the populace, his bedroom, and numerous priceless antiques and artworks. Located at 124 Abercorn Street, it's open Tuesday through Saturday 10:00 A.M. to 5:00 P.M.; Sunday and Monday 2:00 to 5:00 P.M. Admission is charged: adults $3, students $2, ages six to twelve $1, under age six no charge.

On Telfair Square, the Telfair Mansion and Museum, 121 Barnard Street (912–232–1177), is a splendid English Regency masterpiece in its own right. On display are decorative pieces, English and American art and furnishings. It's open Tuesday through Saturday 10:00 A.M. to 5:00 P.M. and Sunday 2:00 to 5:00 P.M. Adults are $2.50; students, $1; age six to twelve, 50¢; free for all on Sunday.

Some of Savannah's most interesting dining experiences—like its landmarks—are a bit off the beaten path. Here are a few local favorites:

Clary's Drug Store on 402 Abercorn Street (912–232–5153) is a neighborhood pharmacy. One side is a lunch counter and collection of tables where locals come Monday through Saturday for morning coffee and Southern breakfast, a meat-and-potatoes lunch, gossip and casual camaraderie. It's very inexpensive, and no credit cards are accepted.

After breakfast or lunch at Clary's, you can step across the street and rent a bike at Chris' Bike Shop, 347 Abercorn Street, (912) 232–5338.

Crystal Beer Parlor, a comfortable old tavern on 301 West Jones Street at Jefferson Street (912–232–1153), has served delicious fried oyster sandwiches, state-of-the-art onion rings, gumbo, hamburgers, and seafood chowder to generations of Savannah-

93

ians and visitors. Children are welcome. It's inexpensive, open Monday through Saturday, and accepts major credit cards.

Garibaldi's Café, 315 West Congress Street, (912) 232–7118, is an Italian café in the artfully rejuvenated Germania firehouse of 1871 where you'll find excellent pasta, veal, seafood, duck, and chicken. Moderately priced dinner is served nightly. Major credit cards are accepted.

Something of a paradox, Mrs. Wilkes Boardinghouse, probably Savannah's best-known dining room, is hidden unpretentiously away in the historic district at 107 West Jones Street, (912) 232–5997. You know you're there by the long lines waiting outside. Family-style lunch includes endless portions of fried chicken, fried fish, barbecue, vegetables, corn bread, biscuits, and dessert. Breakfast features eggs, sausage, biscuits, and buttered grits. Very inexpensive breakfast and lunch are available Monday through Friday; no credit cards are accepted.

Wall's Bar-B-Q, located on York Lane, between East Oglethorpe Avenue and East York Street, (912) 232–9754, is a Savannah institution, humble in appearance but celestial in its output. Specialties include tangy barbecued chicken and pork, ribs, and some of the most delicious deviled crab in this famous seafood city. Open Thursday, Friday, Saturday only, it's very inexpensive (no credit cards).

Reserve the lovely dining room at 45 South, 20 East Broad Street, (912) 354–0444, for your one big dining-out splurge. With its own kitchen and separate entrance in the Pirates' House restaurant complex, 45 South excels in such continental and nouvelle American dishes as angel hair pasta with smoked mussels, roulade of salmon with leeks and light cream, and peppered duck breast with acorn squash. Lunch (moderate) is served Monday to Friday; dinner (expensive), Monday to Saturday. Major credit cards are welcome.

Emma's, 224 West Bay Street, (912) 232–1223, is a wonderful way to wind up a memorable Savannah day. Pianist-songstress Emma Kelly is a beloved Savannah personality who plays the great tunes of the past and a few popular favorites in a living room–like bistro with a cozy dance floor. She's on hand Monday through Saturday.

To experience Savannah's Old World charisma thoroughly, stay overnight in an historic inn or bed and breakfast. More than two dozen are situated in vintage mansions and townhouses, furnished with antiques and artworks. Rates usually include breakfast, afternoon wine or tea, and a late-night liqueur. Some of the most atmospheric include Ballastone Inn, 14 East Oglethorpe Avenue, (912) 236–1484; Bed and Breakfast Inn, 117 West Gordon Street, (912) 238–0518; Comer House, 2 East Taylor Street, (912) 234–2923; East Bay Inn, 225 East Bay Street, (912) 238–1225; Gastonian Inn, 220 East Gaston Street, (912) 232–2869; Magnolia Place Inn, 503 Whitaker Street, (912) 236–2869; and Planters Inn, 29 Abercorn Street, (912) 232–5678. You may make reservations at a dozen inns through a central toll-free number, (800) 262–4667.

Some of Savannah's most intriguing off-the-beaten-path attractions are away from the downtown historic district, on outlying beaches and coastal islands. First head east to Fort Jackson, Fort Pulaski, and the beaches and historic sites on Tybee Island.

Fort Jackson, on Highway 80/Islands Expressway 3 miles east of downtown, was constructed along the Savannah River in various stages between 1808 and 1879. All shipping bound for Savannah's port had to pass by the fort's heavy guns. A tidal moat still girds the sturdy brick walls. Artifacts include cannon, small arms, machinery, and tools that are demonstrated at yearly special events. In summer, cannon firings and military drills are conducted by uniformed soldiers at 1 Fort Jackson Road. The fort (912–233–3945) is open daily 9:00 A.M. to 5:00 P.M. Adults are $2; students, military, and senior citizens, $1.50.

Oatland Island Education Center, just off the Islands Expressway east of the Wilmington River, is a fascinating nature experience for all ages. Operated by the Savannah-Chatham Public Schools, the center is a focus of nature education programs and special activities. Even on a short visit, you may walk through a nature trail and see an astonishing variety of wildlife. In secured natural habitats, you'll observe alligators, wolves, bobcats, bears, panthers, deer, bald eagles, egrets, heron, lizards, and many other creatures. Located at 711 Sandtown Road (912–897–3773), it's open Monday through Friday 8:30 A.M. to 5:00 P.M. and October to May the second Saturday of the month 11 A.M. to 5:00 P.M. There is an admission fee: one can of cat or dog food per person.

Fort Pulaski National Monument, off Highway 80, guards the Savannah River entrance from the Atlantic Ocean. The star-shaped fortress took eighteen years to construct—a young West

Point engineering graduate named Robert E. Lee lent his expertise—but surrendered to Union forces on April 11, 1862, following a brief but devastating attack by the new cannon rifles. Maintained by the National Park Service, the fort's visitors center—Cockspur Island, 15 miles east of downtown, (912) 786–5787—has historical exhibits, weapons, and uniforms. Admission from March 1 to Labor Day is $1 adults, under sixteen and over sixty-two no charge; maximum for carload, $3. The rest of year it's free for all.

There's nothing chic or glamorous about Tybee Island—in truth, it's the very antithesis of rich and fashionable Southern resorts such as South Carolina's Hilton Head Island. And therein lies the charm of this comfortable old shoe of a beach and summer home island, 20 miles east of downtown Savannah. Many Savannah families spend the torrid summers in cottages near the beach, where a mild Atlantic surf laps 3 miles of hard-packed sands.

In warm weather, you'll probably want to make a beeline for one of the Tybee beaches. The most popular locale for swimming and sunbathing is the commercial area around Butler Avenue and 16th Street—a funky, old-fashioned–looking place straight from Coney Island, circa 1940. Here you'll find ice cream and fudge shops, chair and beach umbrella vendors, a fishing pier, small motels and cottages, public rest rooms, and changing rooms and showers. For most of your needs, as the slogan says, "If It's Something You Use, You Can Find It at Chu's." That's T. S. Chu and Co., a Tybee landmark for a half century. Inside you'll find bathing suits, lotions, beachballs, games, and toys. The late founder, Chinese immigrant T. S. Chu, also left his name on many other Tybee businesses.

Throughout the year, don't miss the **Tybee Island Museum and Lighthouse.** Housed inside a Spanish American War coastal artillery battery, the museum is like a trip through an incredible attic. On display are Civil War rifles, flintlock pistols, a pictorial history of the island, old newspapers, magazines, and marriage licenses, a plaster pietà, antique dolls, shrunken heads, ancient armor, homage to Savannah's world-famous songwriter Johnny Mercer, stuffed birds and butterflies, Nazi flags and Japanese samurai swords, an English whiskey still, a World War II exhibit with propaganda leaflets, and a model of the cotton gin that Connecticut Yankee Eli Whitney invented during a 1793 Savannah vacation. You may view the beach from the outdoor observation platform.

You may also climb the spiraling 178 steps to the top of the adjacent lighthouse, which was completed in 1867 and rises 145 feet. After huffing and puffing to the top, you'll be rewarded with scenic views from the observation deck. The museum is open April 1 to September 30, daily 10:00 A.M. to 6:00 P.M. and October 1 to March 31, Monday to Friday 1:00 to 5:00 P.M. and Saturday and Sunday 10:00 A.M. to 5:00 P.M. Adults are $1; ages twelve and under are free when accompanied by an adult; Call (912) 786–4077. The lighthouse (912–786–5801) is open June 1 to August 31, daily 1:00 to 5:00 P.M. and September 1 to May 31, Thursday to Monday 1:00 to 5:00 P.M. Adults are $1; ages six to twelve, 50¢ when accompanied by an adult.

Moderately priced accommodations on the beach include the Days Inn Tybee Island (912–786–4576) and the DeSoto Beach Motel (912–786–4542).

After an energetic day at the beach, head for Williams Seafood, Highway 80 at the Bull River Bridge, (912) 897–2219, for simply prepared fried and broiled seafood at very low prices. It's open for lunch and dinner daily, no credit cards accepted. You may also join swarms of locals and tourists fishing for their sustenance off the bridges.

Skidaway Island, south of downtown, has its own trove of off-the-beaten-path adventures. **Skidaway Island State Park,** off Diamond Causeway, (912) 356–2523, is a 490-acre preserve that's relaxed and quiet even in the busiest seasons. The one hundred tent and trailer camping sites ($8 a night) have water and electrical connections, showers and rest rooms. Amenities include a swimming pool, picnic shelters, nature trails and weekend nature programs, and a playground. There's no beach (or fishing) inside the park, but there are plenty of opportunities for both nearby.

The Skidaway Island Marine Extension Center (912–356–2496), operated by the University of Georgia, includes an excellent small aquarium. The twelve tanks house a colorful array of coastal fish, including moray eels, barracuda, catfish, pigfish, moonfish, pompano, squirrei fish, and porcupine fish. It's open Monday through Friday 9:00 A.M. to 4:00 P.M., and Saturday and Sunday noon to 5:00 P.M. It's on McWhorter Drive, off Diamond Causeway.

At **Wormsloe State Historic Site,** a picturesque and very

Georgia Coast

photogenic 1 1/2-mile avenue of live oaks leads to the tabby ruins of a colonial estate built by Noble Jones, one of the original contingent of settlers who arrived with General James Edward Oglethorpe in 1733. The visitors center displays artifacts excavated on the estate and an audiovisual show about the founding of the Georgia Crown Colony. You may walk a nature trail to the Jones family gravesite and tabby foundations of their eighteenth-century home. During special times of the year such as Christmas season, Memorial Day, Labor Day, and Georgia Week in February, staff in period dress demonstrate colonial crafts and skills. Located at 7601 Skidaway Road (912–352–2548), it's open Tuesday through Saturday 9:00 A.M. to 5:00 P.M. and Sunday 2:00 to 5:30 P.M.

The nearby Isle of Hope is another picturesque place for a drive or walk. Go to the end of LaRoche Avenue and follow Bluff Drive along the Wilmington River. The many lovely homes and a frame Roman Catholic church are set off by towering live oaks and banks of azaleas.

After all this history and sightseeing, you deserve a tasty treat, which you'll find at Byrd's Cookie Shanty, off Skidaway Road and Ferguson Avenue at 2233 Norwood Avenue, (912) 355–1716. The Byrd Cookie Co. was founded in 1924 by Benjamin Byrd, who baked delectable crisp wafers flavored with benne, or sesame, seeds. Today, the thriving little company is run by the founder's son Benjamin "Cookie" Byrd Jr. and his wife. The product line has been increased to include molasses cookies, wild rice tea cakes, pizza-style cocktail snacks, and other treats. If you go to the Cookie Shanty, you'll meet "Cookie" Byrd himself at the ovens and assembly line in the back of the shop. You'll get free samples hot from the oven and the opportunity to chat with this delightful gentleman. You may purchase other goodies at the front counter, Monday through Saturday.

Fort McAllister State Historic Park, 25 miles south of Savannah in Bryan County, is highlighted by the best preserved earthwork fortifications anywhere in the old Confederacy. Built on bluffs above the south bank of the Great Ogeechee River, the earthworks withstood seven Union land and sea assaults before finally capitulating in December 1864. It was the last major obstacle on General William T. Sherman's "March to the Sea" and led to Savannah's peaceful surrender shortly thereafter. The earthworks and heavy guns have been restored to their wartime appearance. The museum and visitors center has Civil War weapons and other artifacts.

Also part of Fort McAllister is a recreation area (912–727–2339) with seventy-five tent and trailer camping sites ($8 a night), with electricity, water, rest rooms and showers, picnic tables and grills, 5 miles of hiking trails, boat ramps, and docks. To get there, follow Highway 144, 10 miles east of Interstate 95's exit 15.

To or from the fort, stop for a delicious seafood lunch or dinner at Love's Seafood Restaurant, Highway 17 at the Ogeechee River bridge. The dining room overlooks the river; prices are inexpensive. Lunch is served daily except Saturday, dinner nightly. Major credit cards are accepted.

Liberty County

As you drive along Highway 17 between Savannah and Brunswick, **Midway Church** looms out of the gnarled arms of a live oak grove, looking like a New England meetinghouse that's lost its way. In fact, the white clapboard church, with its gabled roof and square belfry, traces its heritage to Massachusetts Puritans, who founded the Midway Society in 1754. The present church dates from 1792. Illustrious parishioners have included two signers of the Declaration of Independence and Theodore Roosevelt's great-grandfather. The fathers of Oliver Wendell Holmes and Samuel F. B. Morse have served as pastor.

Pick up the big iron key at the Gulf station. The church interior has straightback pews, slaves gallery, and unadorned walls. Across the highway, the churchyard is the resting place of Midway's founders and Revolutionary heroes. The adjacent Midway Museum, open Tuesday through Saturday 9:00 A.M. to 5:00 P.M. and Sunday 2:00 to 5:30 P.M., (912) 884–5837, has colonial furnishings, documents, and exhibits. Adults are $1; ages twelve and under, 50¢.

You can really forsake the beaten path by taking Highway 38 14 miles east of Midway, to the site of **Sunbury.** The curator at the small museum will relate the history of this vanished colonial seaport and point out the ruins of Fort Morris, a bulwark against British attack during the Revolution and War of 1812.

West of Midway, via Highway 82, the Military Museum (912–767–4891), at the U.S. Army's Fort Stewart, displays uniforms, weapons, flags, photos, and vehicles from the Civil War through

Vietnam. It's open Monday through Friday, 1:00 to 5:00 P.M.; Saturday and Sunday 2:00 to 6:00 P.M. Stimulated by Fort Stewart's large payroll, nearby Hinesville is full of motels, shopping centers, and restaurants serving everything from fast food and American dishes to German, Chinese, Mexican, and Korean cuisine.

McIntosh County

This coastal county, between Savannah and Brunswick, was the site of a British fort that predated Georgia's founding as a colony in 1733. Marshy bays and coastal islands are home of national marine and wildlife refuges and picturesque fleets of fishing boats and shrimping trawlers.

Stop first at the Darien Welcome Center (912–437–6684), on Highway 17 at the Altamaha River bridge for general information and reservations for Sapelo Island tours. The **Fort King George State Historic Site,** a mile off Highway 17, (912) 437–4770, marks an earthwork and pallisaded log fortress built by South Carolinians in 1721 to fend off Spanish advances from Florida. Most of the fort was destroyed by fire in 1726.

A state visitors center and museum has displays, artifacts, and a film of the fort and early Georgia life and is open Tuesday through Saturday 9:00 A.M. to 5:00 P.M. and Sunday 2:00 to 5:30 P.M. Adults are $1; ages six to twelve, 50¢. On the way to the fort site, you may stop and photograph Darien's shrimp fleet and St. Cyprian's Episcopal Church (1870) Darien's first black house of worship.

Open Gates Bed & Breakfast, Vernon Square, Darien 31305, (912) 437–6985, is a gem of a country inn. Every room in the century-old home is like a page from a glossy home-and-garden magazine. Owners Carolyn and Philip Hodges have embellished guest rooms with American and European antiques, family heirlooms and portraits, handmade quilts and china. The house is comfortably air-conditioned and has a small swimming pool. The Hodges are a wealth of information about off-the-beaten-path places to visit and photograph. Rates of $50 double include an ample continental breakfast.

From Darien, Highway 99 meanders 16.3 miles along the marshes, low country, and fishing villages that make McIntosh County special. At Meridian, you'll catch the state-operated ferry to Sapelo Island. Go north another 1.6 miles, look for a sign to

Valona, a few docks, and a post office with plenty of opportunities to photograph the shrimping trawlers. (Valona was named for an Albanian fishing port!)

Highway 99 loops back into Highway 17 and Interstate 95 at Eulonia. At South Newport, north of Eulonia, you can "Rub Elbows With God" at what's purportedly the smallest church in America. Christ Chapel seats twelve for services every third Sunday. The stained-glass windows were imported from England.

Sapelo Island Tours, conducted by the Georgia Department of Natural Resources, take you through the fascinating ecology of the Sapelo Island National Estuarine Sanctuary. On the thirty-minute ferry trip from Meridian, you'll skirt wavering stands of cord grass marsh, scores of small islets and hammocks. Touring the island on a school bus, see the exterior of a mansion built by tobacco baron R. J. Reynolds. Naturalists will show you how to seine a flounder, explain some of the mysteries of the marshes, and point out deer, wild turkeys, and many species of waterfowl that call the island home. You'll have forty-five minutes to walk the beaches and collect shells. The island's facilities are limited to rest rooms, water fountains, and soft drink machines. Bring a snack, if you wish, and don't forget the insect repellent!

Four-hour tours are conducted every Wednesday and Friday (leaving Meridian at 8:30 A.M., returning at 12:30 P.M.) and on Saturday from 9:00 A.M. to 1:00 P.M. A more extensive tour—8:30 A.M. to 3:00 P.M.—is conducted once a month from March through October. Required reservations are made through the Darien Welcome Center, Box 734, Darien 31305, (912) 437–6684. No tickets are sold at the Meridian dock. It costs $5, with no charge for those under age six.

Hofwyl-Broadfield Rice Plantation, on U.S. Highway 17, 6 miles south of Darien, is a reminder of the rice culture that once flourished along the Altamaha River. Stop by the state parks visitors center and view the slide presentation, then take a 1-mile walking tour above the overgrown rice fields and to the main house. The plantation was owned by one family from 1806 to 1973, and the simple white frame house, circa 1850, has many original furnishings.

It's open Tuesday through Saturday 9:00 A.M. to 5:00 P.M. and Sunday 2:00 to 5:30 P.M. Adults are $1.50; ages six to twelve, 75¢; under age five, no charge.

You can feast on marvelous McIntosh County seafood on or well off the beaten path. The most obvious place is Archie's Restaurant, on Highway 17 in Darien, (912) 437–4363, which serves fried oysters, shrimp and scallops, flounder, crabs and hushpuppies for lunch and dinner Monday through Saturday. Speed's Kitchen (912–832–4763), off Highway 17 near Eulonia, requires some directions but is worth the search. First-rate seafoods are served at Sunday lunch and dinner Thursday, Friday, Saturday.

Glynn County

"The Golden Isles" are a necklace of lush, subtropical barrier islands that serpentine languidly along Georgia's Atlantic coast for more than 120 miles. Several of the principal islands accessible to visitors are part of Glynn County. Even the most highly developed islands—St. Simons and Jekyll—are low-key, laid back, and lightly commercialized when compared with other resort islands along the Eastern Seaboard. And with their long stretches of beaches, marshes, inlets, rivers, and live oak forests it's very easy to get off the beaten path and commune in solitude with untrampled nature.

Brunswick, the Glynn County seat and a center of Georgia's shrimping and oystering industries, is the gateway to Jekyll, St. Simons, Sea, and Little St. Simons islands. Like Savannah, Brunswick was laid out in the eighteenth century on a precise grid, with public squares at regular intervals. Included on the National Register of Historic Places since 1978, many homes and public buildings on Union, Reynolds, Egmont, Prince, London, Dartmouth, and other British-sounding streets date back to the early-and mid-nineteenth century. Gingerbreaded and wrought-iron–trimmed showplaces in Queen Anne, Gothic, Italianate, Mansard, and Jacobean styles are enhanced by towering live oaks, banks of azaleas, and dogwoods and camellias.

Pick up a driving tour map at the **Old Town Preservation Association** offices in the Old City Hall downtown on Gloucester Street, (912) 264–0442. The turreted Queen Anne–style City Hall dates back to 1883. The Glynn County Courthouse, nearby at Reynolds and G streets, is one of the Southeast's most beautiful. The classical building, topped by a cupola, sits in the midst of a mini-botanical garden of moss-draped live oaks, Chinese pistachio, magnolia, and swamp holly trees, and flowering shrubbery.

Young ladies in your entourage will especially enjoy the **Mary Miller Doll Museum,** 1523 Glynn Avenue (912–267–7569). The museum's more than 4,000 dolls include pre–Civil War china heads, bisques, early vinyls, carved woodens, foreign dolls, antique travel cases, and hundreds of dresses and accessories. Open Monday through Saturday 11:00 A.M. to 5:00 P.M. Adults are $1.50; ages seven to fifteen, $1, under age seven, no charge.

If you'd like to try your hand at deep sea fishing or just get out on the open sea for a spell of quiet relaxation, you'll find numerous boats available for charter around the Brunswick docks at the end of Gloucester Street. Check with the Brunswick–Golden Isles Tourist and Convention Bureau, 4 Glynn Avenue, Brunswick 31520, (912) 265–0620, for specifics.

The Brunswick–Golden Isles Welcome Center (912–264–5337), at Highway 17 and the St. Simons Causeway, has a thirteen-minute audiovisual orientation to the area, maps, brochures, and information about activities, lodgings, and special interests.

When hunger strikes, follow the natives to Kody's Restaurant (912–267–1407), downtown at 300 Gloucester Street, for inexpensive Southern and coastal dishes at breakfast, lunch, and dinner Monday through Friday.

The Captain's Table (912–265–2549), Highway 17 north, also specializes in coastal seafoods at inexpensive to moderate prices at daily lunch, dinner, and Sunday brunch.

You can also buy shrimp, oysters, blue crabs, flounder, and other fish fresh off the boats and prepare them yourself.

A causeway ($1 per car) connects Brunswick with Jekyll Island. Stop first at the Jekyll Island Welcome Center, at the island end of the causeway, (912) 635–3636; toll-free in Georgia (800) 342–1042; outside (800) 841–6586. It's open daily 9:00 A.M. to 5:00 P.M.

Between 1886 and 1942, Jekyll was the winter home of some of America's richest and most illustrious families. From the Gilded Age until the beginning of World War II, Astors, Pulitzers, Vanderbilts, Morgans, Rockefellers, Cranes, Goodyears, and other aristocrats lived in secluded luxury on this remote Georgia island. Shortly after Pearl Harbor, they boarded up their elegant "cottages" and left the island for the last time. After the war, the state of Georgia paid $675,000 for the island and turned it into a state park.

One side of the island is skirted by nearly 10 miles of hard-packed Atlantic beaches, washed by a mild surf that's perfect for small children and waders. Free showers, rest rooms, and changing rooms are at regular intervals along the beachfront. Even on the busiest holiday weekends, there's plenty of room to get away from everybody else. The other side is flanked by the Intracoastal Waterway and scenic salt marshes. Deer, raccoon, armadillo, and wild turkey roam live oak, magnolia, and pine forests.

Tours of the **Jekyll Island Club Historic District** begin at the Museum Orientation Center. View the free audiovisual presentation before setting off for a ninety-minute tour in a motorized tram. Highlights include Faith Chapel's stained-glass windows signed by Louis Comfort Tiffany and "Indian Mound," William Rockefeller's shingled Cape Cod–style cottage. Tours are conducted daily from Memorial Day to Labor Day at 10:00 A.M., noon, 2:00 and 4:00 P.M.; Labor Day to Memorial Day, 10:00 A.M., noon, 2:00 P.M. Adults are $6; ages six to eighteen, $4; under age six, no charge.

In addition to the beach, Jekyll's recreational outlets include sixty-three holes of golf, indoor and outdoor tennis, rental bikes, fishing, a water slide and wave pool park, picnic grounds, and hiking.

Lodgings include campgrounds with water and electrical hookups; six hotels widely spaced along the beachfront; and the glamorous and deluxe Jekyll Club Hotel on the Intracoastal Waterway. In the island's "Golden Age," the Jekyll Club was the millionaires' dining area, social center, and guest lodgings. A $20-million restoration has brought it splendidly back to life. Even if you're not staying there, walk through the lobbies and public rooms and admire the stained glass, plaster moulding, and other rich architectural details. Contact the hotel at 371 Riverview Drive, Jekyll Island 31520; toll-free outside Georgia (800) 822-1886, inside Georgia (800) 843–5355. It's very expensive.

St. Simons Island, also reached by causeway from Brunswick, is the most popular of the "Golden Isles," but hotels, shopping, and other tourist amenities haven't dimmed the natural splendor of live oaks, salt marshes, beaches, and stately live oaks veiled in Spanish moss. On the island you may swim and sunbathe on long strands of beaches—all Georgia beaches are public domain—fish, ride horseback, and enjoy historic sites dating back to the early eighteenth century.

Fort Frederica National Monument, at the island's north

ern end, includes remnants of a fortress built by the British in the early 1730s as a guardian against Spanish attack from Florida. Leading up to the fort are the foundations of homes and shops occupied by 1,500 soldiers and civilians. The fort was never tested. The Spanish did come, in 1742, and their defeat at the nearby Battle of Bloody Marsh left England firmly in control of Georgia's coast. Stop first at the National Park Service Visitors Center (912–638–3639) for a film and historical displays. It's open daily 9:00 A.M. to 5:00 P.M. Adults are $1; children, 50¢.

Christ Church, a Gothic wooden structure on the road to Fort Frederica, is the island's most beloved landmark. The site of services conducted by John and Charles Wesley for Frederica's garrison, the original church was built in 1820. Desecrated by Union soldiers, it was rebuilt in 1884 by the Reverend Anson Phelps Didge, whose life was chronicled by St. Simons resident Eugenia Price's novel *Beloved Invader.* Framed by an arbor of live oaks, dogwoods, and azaleas, the interior is illuminated by stained-glass windows. It's open daily; donations are welcome. Episcopal services are conducted on Sunday.

At the south end of the island, near the causeway entrance, **St. Simons Lighthouse** has been a landmark since 1872. The Museum of Coastal History in the lightkeeper's cottage displays collections of colonial furniture, shipbuilding tools, and changing exhibitions of coastal art. It's open Tuesday to Saturday 1:00 to 4:00 P.M. and Sunday 1:30 to 4:30 P.M. Adults are $1.50; ages six to twelve, $1.

Neptune Park, around the lighthouse, has seaside picnic tables, a playground, and steps down to the beach. You can surf fish from the beach or take a cooler and lawn chair onto the Municipal Pier and angle for flounder and whiting and even pull up a startled hammerhead shark or barracuda on occasion. No license is required for saltwater fishing.

Massingale Beach, on Ocean Boulevard, between the King & Prince Hotel and the U.S. Coast Guard Station, has free showers, rest rooms, picnic tables, and a snack bar just off the beach. Don't be disappointed because the Atlantic isn't brilliant turquoise and emerald. Rivers emptying into the ocean give it a silt rather than a sand bottom and turn the waters grayish green.

If you're on a budget, make reservations at Queen's Court, an old-fashioned but clean and comfortable motel with some kitch-

Jekyll Island Club House

enette rooms near the lighthouse and Neptune Park at 437 Kings Way, St. Simons Island 31522, (912) 638–8459.

Epworth-by-the-Sea, a Methodist conference center, spiritual retreat, and vacation center has 600 modern motel rooms, an inexpensive cafeteria, tennis, fishing, and swimming at moderate rates. You don't have to be Methodist, but alcohol, unmarried couples, and rowdy behavior aren't tolerated. Write to the center at Box 407, St. Simons Island 31522 or call (912–638–8688).

For the most authentic taste of old St. Simons, plan dinner at Alfonza's Olde Plantation Supper Club, Harrington Lane, off Frederica Road (912) 638–9883. The low-ceilinged room is heavy with coastal atmosphere and serves delicious local shrimp, oysters, crab, and flounder. It's open for dinner Monday to Saturday at moderate prices.

The Crab Trap, 1209 Ocean Boulevard, (912) 638–3552, is a casual seafood shack with fried and broiled seafoods and draft beer. It's open nightly for dinner, at inexpensive prices.

The world is truly not much with us at Little St. Simons Island. By the time we've made the twenty-minute launch crossing from "big" St. Simons, the world's problems have vanished in the sunlight of another glorious coastal morning. A fortunate set of circumstances has left the island—6 miles long by 2 to 3 miles wide—very nearly as nature created it.

Through the 1800s, the 10,000 acres were the domain of one rice planter and his descendants. In 1903, a pencil company purchased the island, but when the red cedars proved too wind-twisted for writing instruments, it became an off-the-beaten-path retreat, now open to the public.

Guests stay in rustically comfortable lodges that accommodate up to twenty-four. They dine at communal tables and spend their days on 6 miles of wild beaches; crabbing and fishing; taking nature walks into forests inhabited by deer, raccoon, armadillo, pelicans, red-tail hawks, great blue heron, egret, and more than 200 other species, and alongside marshes and rivers where gators like ironclad vessels cruise.

Full American Plan rates of $250 a couple a night include all meals, fishing, beach and pool swimming, horseback riding, and transportation from St. Simons Island. Contact Little St. Simons Island, P.O. Box 1078, St. Simons Island 31522, (912) 638–7472.

Sea Island, connected to St. Simons Island by a small bridge, is the home of the renowned Cloister Hotel, one of America's legendary resorts. Even if you're not a guest, you may admire the beautifully landscaped grounds and drive by the stately homes lining Sea Island Drive. Non-guests may also play the Cloister's Sea Island Golf Course and tennis courts and have lunch or dinner in the dining rooms. Contact Sea Island 31561, (912) 638–3611. It's very expensive.

Camden County

Southernmost of Georgia's Atlantic coastal counties, Camden is the jumping-off place for the Cumberland Island National Seashore. It's also home for U.S. Navy's Kings Bay Trident Submarine base.

Stretching 18 miles long, by 1 to 2 miles wide, Cumberland is by far the largest of Georgia's barrier islands, and of those open to the public, the most primeval. Like a savory dish, blended of many exotic ingredients, **Cumberland Island National Seashore** is an intricate web of nature's rarest, most wondrous gifts. Preserved as a National Seashore since 1972, maintained by the National Park Service, it holds an astonishing treasure of marshes and dunes, pristine beaches, live oak forests, lakes, ponds, estuaries, and inlets.

"Natives" include great blue heron, wood storks, egrets, and dozens of other bird species, many of them rarely seen beyond these shores; giant sea turtles, which plod over the beaches to renew their race; fiddler, hermit and ghost crabs, shrimp, oysters, and flounder; deer, armadillo, mink, wild horses, and wild boar; playful otters, cruising gators.

Mankind's 4,000-year habitation began with ancient Guale Indians, followed by sixteenth-century Spanish missionaries, eighteenth-century British troops, and pre–Civil War rice, indigo and cotton planters. Thomas Carnegie, of the Pittsburgh Carnegies, bought the entire island in the 1880s. His family's splendid estates were mostly abandoned when the "Gilded Age" gave way to the "Roaring Twenties," and high society discovered more fashionable wintering destinations. With only a few intrusions, the island has passed into public trust largely as it was created.

Unless you own your own boat, the only way to enjoy Cumberland's glories is via a forty-five-minute ride on *The Cumberland Queen* from St. Marys. With a capacity of 150, the ferry departs daily from mid-May through Labor Day at 9:00 A.M., arriving Cumberland at 9:45, and 11:45 A.M. arriving Cumberland at 12:30. It departs Cumberland at 10:15 A.M., arriving at St. Marys at 11:00, and 4:45 P.M., arriving St. Marys at 5:30. The rest of the year, it operates at the same times daily except Tuesday and Wednesday. Including taxes, fares are $7.88 adults; age sixty-five and over, $6.57; twelve and under, $4.05.

Reservations may be made up to eleven months in advance by contacting Cumberland Island National Seashore, P.O. Box 806, St. Marys 31558, (912) 882–4335. Bear in mind that sailing times are exact. If you miss the last ferry from the island, you'll have to hire a boat from St. Marys or Fernandina Beach, Florida.

Campers have a choice of developed and primitive campgrounds. Sea Camp, a five-minute walk from the ferry dock, has bathrooms and hot showers; primitive camp sites, a 3 1/2-to 10-mile hike from the dock, have trench latrines and cold water spigots.

If you're a day-tripper, you can hike several nature trails, swim and sun, and view the remains of the Carnegie estates. Park Service rangers lead history and nature walks. There's nothing at all for sale on the island, so remember to bring food, cold drinks, insect repellent, and sunscreen.

The island's only hotel-type lodgings are at the Greyfield Inn, a Carnegie family home. Guests sleep in four-poster beds, bathe in claw-footed tubs, and relax amid family portraits and mementoes. The unique experience costs $85 to $95 a person per night, plus 5 percent sales tax and 15 percent gratuity, and $15 round-trip service on the Inn's ferry from Fernandina Beach, Florida. All meals are included. Contact, Drawer B, Fernandina Beach, FL 32034, (904) 261–6408.

The Riverview Hotel, across from the Park Service docks in St. Marys, has comfortable, air-conditioned rooms for $39 a double. The hotel's Seagle's Restaurant—105 Osborne Street, St. Marys 31558, (912) 882–3242—serves breakfast, local seafoods, steaks, beer, cocktails at moderate prices.

Crooked River State Park, outside St. Marys, has a swimming pool, fishing, playgrounds, camp sites ($8 a night), and cottages ($45 a night, Sunday through Thursday, $55 Friday and Saturday). Contact 3092 Spur 40, St. Marys 31558, (912) 882–5256.

Off the Beaten Path in Northeast Georgia

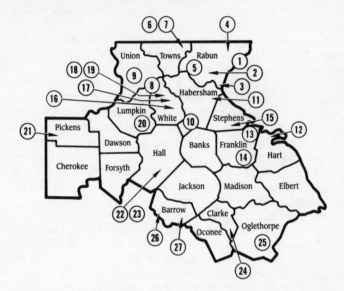

1. Chattooga River Rafting
2. Rabun Beach Recreation Area
3. Tallulah Gorge/Terrora Park
4. Black Rock Mountain State Park
5. Mocassin Creek State Park
6. Georgia Mountain Fair
7. Brasstown Bald Mountain
8. Richard Russell Scenic Highway
9. Vogel State Park
10. Habersham Vineyards
11. Mark of the Potter
12. Hart State Park
13. Tugaloo State Park
14. Victoria Bryant State Park
15. Travelers Rest/Toccoa Falls
16. Babyland General Hospital/Mount Yonah
17. Old Sautee Store/Stovall Covered Bridge
18. "Alpine Helen"
19. Unicoi State Park/Anna Ruby Falls
20. Dahlonega Courthouse Gold Museum/Crisson's Mine
21. Amicalola Falls State Park/Appalachian Trail approach trail
22. Lake Lanier Islands
23. Gainesville Green Street Historical District
24. Athens of Old Tours/State Botanical Garden
25. Watson Mill Bridge State Park
26. Chateau Elan Winery
27. Fort Yargo State Park

Northeast Georgia

Depending on which direction you've set your hiking boots, the 2,015-mile Appalachian Trial either begins or ends with 79 miles of northeast Georgia mountainland. Many AT veterans acclaim the Georgia section as the most beautiful in all the fourteen states between here and Mount Katahdin, Maine.

The AT's southern terminus is atop 3,782-foot Springer Mountain, in Dawson County, 75 miles northeast of Atlanta. An 8-mile approach trail begins at Amicalola Falls State Park. There, hikers may camp out, get their gear together, and have their packs weighed by park rangers. The 400-acre park, centered on a majestic 729-foot waterfall, is an outdoor destination in its own right, with hiking trails above and below the falls, picnic areas, fishing, camp sites ($8 a night)—with electricity, water, hot showers, and rest rooms—and furnished cottages with fireplaces ($45 a night Sunday through Thursday, $55 Friday and Saturday). Contact the park superintendent, Star Route, Dawsonville 30534, (404) 265–2885.

From Springer Mountain, the AT's Section I is a 22.3-mile easy-to-strenuous hike to Highway 60 at Woody Gap. Section II, 10.7 miles from Woody Gap to Neels Gap, has just one long uphill stretch and is popular with one-day and weekend hikers. At Neels Gap, the trail crosses Highway 19/129 and goes "indoors" as it passes through a covered breezeway of the Mountain Crossing/Walasi-Yi Center. At this stone and log legacy of the 1930s Civilian Conservation Corps (CCC), hikers can get trail information and replenish supplies of dehydrated foods and camping gear. Motorists stop by for mountain handicrafts and cold cider and short hikes on the trail. From Walasi-Yi, Section III is a moderately difficult 5.7 miles to Tesnatee Gap on the Richard Russell Scenic Highway (Highway 348). Sections IV–VI carry the trail upwards and onwards. At Bly Gap, near the Rabun County/Towns County border, you bid adieu to Georgia and cross into the North Carolina Great Smokies. Mount Katahdin, here we come!

Rabun County

In Georgia's far northeast corner, up against the North Carolina and South Carolina borders, Rabun County is the heart of the state's dramatically rugged Blue Ridge Mountain country. About

80 percent of the county is included in national forests and state parks. Your choice of outdoor adventures ranges from tranquil trout fishing in mountain streams, canoeing, swimming, off-the-beaten-path hiking, and browsing for handmade crafts at country stores to the ultimate heart-pounding adventure: **Chattooga River Rafting.**

Until the early 1970s, when Jon Voigt, Burt Reynolds, and the rest of the *Deliverance* movie crew let the world in on the secret, the Chattooga River was the remote domain of mountain folk along the Georgia–South Carolina border. Nowadays, daredevils come from early spring through late fall to test their courage against the river's steep sluices, whirlpools, and roller-coaster rapids. To see that they accomplish their mission safely, the U.S. Forest Service licenses professional outfitters to conduct the trips, which are made in sturdy six-person rubber rafts, led by guides who know every rock and rill along this tempestuous waterway.

Outfitters such as Wildwater Ltd., Box 100, Long Creek, South Carolina 29658, (803) 647–9587, offer a variety of Chattooga experiences. Beginners usually test their wings on Section III, a seven-hour, 6-mile ride that sweeps them through many of the *Deliverance* landmarks. At lunchtime, guides pull a small deli out of their waterproof packs and spread the feast at the foot of a waterfall. Weekday trips are $36 a person, weekends $40.

Section III is a mere warmup for "The Ultimate Challenge," the Chattooga's wild and wooly Section IV. Suggested only for well-seasoned white-water hands in top physical condition, this rip-snorting seven-hour cruise carries you through swiftly moving currents; steep, wooded gorges; up and over, down and around such potential perils as Seven Foot Falls, Corkscrew, and Jawbone. At day's end, the Chattooga finally turns you loose, into the peaceful waters of Tugaloo Lake. Weekday trips are $46 a person, $55 weekends.

For those who really want to get to the heart of the river, Wildwater Ltd. and other outfitters offer two-day trips, which include overnight camping, a steak dinner, and a bountiful breakfast. Some packages offer the option of lodgings at rustic inns and cabins. Rates range from $99 to $127 a person.

If the Chattooga sparks memories of *Deliverance,* Lake Rabun, near the little town of Tallulah Falls, may remind you of the film *On Golden Pond.* Ringed by the soft green humps of the Blue Ridge Mountains and unpretentious summer cottages, some dating back to the 1920s and '30s, this small off-the-beaten-path lake is the embodiment of peace and quiet. Built in 1922, the Lake Rabun Hotel is the perfect complement to the lake.

Sixteen guest rooms in the wood-and-stone lodge are filled with handmade mountain laurel and rhododendron furniture. With a couple of exceptions, bathrooms are down the hall. You'll have to stay elsewhere for a TV, telephone, central heat, and air-conditioning. The only meal is early morning coffee and dough-nuts by the fireplace. What the Lake Rabun does offer is a rare sweetness and hospitality that draws regulars back year after year. In the evenings, they sit by the flagstone hearth, play parlors games, swap tips on local eateries and "secret" waterfalls and nature trails, and store up energy for the next day's boating, fish-ing, and hiking. Doubles are about $38. Personal checks are ac-cepted, but no credit cards. The hotel is open from the first of April to the end of October. Contact Lake Rabun Hotel, Lakemont 30522, (404) 782-4946.

Fishing boats and canoes may be rented at Hall's Boat House, next to the hotel. The Lake Rabun Road, which twists and turns about 15 miles between Highway 441 near Tallulah Falls, to GA Hwy 197, is a very scenic drive. It curves around Lake Rabun and Seed Lake, with many lovely vistas of the water and woodlands. Ask the proprietors of the Lake Rabun Hotel for directions to High Branch Falls, also known as Minnehaha Falls. It's a little tricky to find but well worth the search. During summer, **Rabun Beach Recreation Area,** a state-run facility, is a relaxing place to swim and have a picnic.

Old Highway 441, a curvy two-lane road running north and south between the Lake Rabun crossroads of Lakemont and the Rabun County seat of Clayton, is another picturesque drive. You may stop for a relaxing Southern-style breakfast, lunch, or dinner at the Green Shutters Inn (404-782-3342), a pretty little place with an antique shop upstairs from the dining room, between Clayton and the community of Tiger.

The Clayton Welcome Center (404-782-5113), on Highway 441, can give you further tips on off-the-beaten-path adventures. You may also contact the Rabun County Chamber of Commerce, Box 761, Clayton 30525; (404) 782-4812.

It may be difficult to imagine now, but early in this century, Tallulah Falls was one of the South's most popular summer re-sorts. Honeymooners, families, and other nature-loving city folk came to admire the cataracts of the Tallulah River, which stormed through a gorge 820 feet across, more than 1,200 feet deep. All that ended in the early 1920s, when a series of hydroelectric dams diverted water from the falls but at the same time created Lake Rabun, Lake Burton, and other recreational areas.

You may stop at the bridge on Highway 441 and stare down at the dam and the depths of the **Tallulah Gorge.** You may also ponder the steely nerves of Karl Wallenda as he tiptoed a tightrope across the gorge in 1970. Pottery, weaving, handmade quilts, jams, preserves, and other handicrafts are sold at several shops around the town of 200.

The Tallulah Gallery (404-754-6020) has a beautiful selection of paintings, pottery, weaving, and other mountain handicrafts in the parlors of a Victorian mansion built by the president of the now-extinct local railroad. The two-story home is on Highway 441 in the center of the small community. Open daily.

Off Highway 441 north of the town and gorge area, **Terrora Park** and Visitors Center, (404) 754–6036, invites you to enjoy an invigorating swim in the Tallulah Lake, go fishing and boating, camp out, and turn the youngsters loose in the playground. Exhibits in the visitors center explain Georgia Power Company's efforts to conserve natural resources.

For the ultimate in rustic mountain lodgings and some of Georgia's most accomplished home cooking, head for LaPrade's, a cluster of cabins, a dining room and fishing docks on Highway 197 at Lake Burton. Built in the early 1920s, the spartan pine cabins have full kitchens and bathrooms and sleep up to twelve. Meals are served family-style, all-you-can eat, at long communal tables in the screened-in dining room.

Breakfast is highlighted by country ham and sausage, hot biscuits and sorghum syrup, grits and eggs. Chicken and dumplings, barbecue, meatloaf, vegetables and corn bread are served at weekday lunch. Some of the world's finest Southern fried chicken is the centerpiece of Sunday lunch and weekday dinner.

You may have all those meals, plus your cabin, for $26 a person a day. If you're just dropping by at mealtime, breakfast is $5.50, lunch $6.50, dinner and Sunday lunch $8.75. Children three to nine dine half-price, under age three free. The dining room is closed Tuesday and Wednesday. Contact LaPrade's, Highway 197 north, Clarkesville 30523; (404) 947–3312.

The Dillard House Inn (404–746–5348) in a beautiful mountain valley off Highway 441 at Dillard, is also renowned for its vast family-style breakfast, lunch, and dinner.

The York House, at nearby Mountain City, is a serene mountain bed and breakfast, with shaded verandas looking over pines and hardwoods and the hazy blue silhouette of the highlands. The fourteen guest rooms are furnished with country antiques and private baths. Rates of about $65 double include a full Southern breakfast. *Deliverance* fans might recall that the film's final scenes took place at the York House, which is not far from the launching place for Chattooga trips. Contact the York House P.O. Box 126, Mountain City 30562, (404) 746–2068.

Two scenic state parks in Rabun County offer a wealth of out-door activities and overnight lodgings. **Black Rock Mountain,** 1,500 acres of brawny beauty atop a 3,600-foot elevation of the Blue Ridge Mountains, has an eighteen-acre lake, many miles of wooded nature trails, waterfalls, camp sites with electrical and water hookups ($8 a night), and furnished cabins with fireplaces and kitchens ($45 Sunday to Thursday, $55 Friday and Saturday). Contact park superintendent, Black Rock Mountain, Mountain City 30562; (404) 746–2141.

Mocassin Creek State Park, on Lake Burton, has a boat ramp and docks, a trout hatchery, hiking trails, and camp sites. Contact park superintendent, Moccasin Creek State Park, Route 1, Lake Burton, Clarkesville 30523; (404) 947–3194.

Towns County

For twelve days early every August, the normally unhurried Towns County seat of Hiawassee (population 1,985) throbs with the energy of the **Georgia Mountain Fair.** Against a backdrop of Blue Ridge Mountains, forests, and blue-green lakes, the fair takes Hiawassee and the rest of Georgia's "Little Switzerland" literally by storm.

The fairgrounds resound with the music of bluegrass fiddlers, gospel singers, clog dancers, and some of the very big names of the country music entertainment world. Scores of craftsmen show off their skills at woodworking, pottery, cornshuck and ap-plehead dolls, painting, leatherwork, furniture and toy making, jewelry, basket weaving, needlework, quilting, and macrame.

Pioneer Village is like a walk through a mountain town of yesteryear. You can peruse the canned goods and bolt cloth in the mercantile store, see the hickory switch in the one-room school-house, the smokehouse and the hand-hewn log cabin. Elsewhere on the forty-two-acre grounds, you can taste just-squeezed apple cider and see a "moonshine" whiskey still up close. "Revenooers" keep a close guard against any free samples.

The annual Cloggers Convention is one of the Mountain Fair's hottest tickets. Groups come from across the South to compete for the top prizes in this synchronized, toe-tapping, very fast-moving musical exercise. Dancers' shoes are equipped with big metal plates that give a clackety-clack rhythm to music from bluegrass to pop and classical. Women cloggers traditionally swirl the floor in short, colorful skirts, buoyed by many layers of stiffly starched petticoats. Men dancers wear jeans and bright gingham shirts. For information, contact Towns County Chamber of Commerce, P.O. Box 290, Hiawassee 30546, (404) 896–4966.

Most of the year, Lake Chatuge is a great place to play. The 7,500-acre Tennessee Valley Authority (TVA) reservoir on the western edge of Hiawassee is a tranquil retreat for trout and bass fishermen, waterskiers, swimmers, and boaters. Several marinas and public boat docks offer easy access to the lake. You'll also find picnic grounds, tennis courts, a sand beach, playgrounds, and camping sites at the 160-acre Towns County Park on the lakeside.

The Chattahoochee National Forest blankets much of Towns County with Georgia pines and hardwoods. Sections of four national wilderness areas in the county afford you the opportunity to get well off the beaten track. During certain times of the year, the Appalachian Trail, crossing Towns County near Brasstown Bald Mountain, gets down-right busy as hikers test their stamina on the 2,300-mile Maine-to-Georgia route described at the beginning of this chapter.

At **Brasstown Bald Mountain**—see "Richard Russell Scenic Highway"—you may follow the 5¹/₂-mile Arkaquah Trail from the crest to Trackrock Gap and the less-strenuous 2¹/₂-mile Jack's Trail Knob to the foot of Brasstown. Wagon Train Road meanders 6 miles to a pastoral valley that cradles the pretty town of Young Harris and the campus of Young Harris College.

Deer Lodge, a hideaway near the junction of highways 66 and 75, is a heaven-sent place to park awhile and savor the glories of the mountains. Hospitable proprietors Richard and Willene Haigler serve some of the biggest, best, and lowest-priced steaks

117

and trout anywhere in these parts. Cabins secluded in the nearby woods are about $25 a night. Contact Deer Lodge, Hiawassee 30546, (404) 896–2726.

Union and White Counties

The **Richard Russell Scenic Highway,** in White and Union counties, takes you through the heart of some of northeast Georgia's most spectacular mountain country. Designated as Highway 348, the 14-mile paved highway takes you from the outskirts of Georgia's "Alpine Village" of Helen, across the Appalachian Trail, to the state's highest mountain and a picture postcard state park. Several parking areas and overlooks give you the chance to stop and admire the rugged beauty of the Blue Ridge Mountains. The drive is especially striking in mid-October to early November, when hardwoods turn brilliantly orange, yellow, and scarlet.

One of the Scenic Highway's "high points" is 3,137-foot Tesnatee Gap, where the Appalachian Trail crosses on its way between Maine and Springer Mountain, Georgia. You can get out of your car here and mingle awhile with the earnest hikers. At its northwestern end, the Scenic Highway intersects with Highway 180. If you turn right, you may explore 4,784-foot Brasstown Bald. A steep, paved road ends at a parking area 930 feet below the summit. From here, either hike to the crest of Georgia's highest peak or take a commercial van up to the view of four states.

A left turn at Highway 180 will lead you to Highway 19 and **Vogel State Park.** Cradled in mountains, beside a pretty lake, Vogel is a delightful place for fishing, boating, warm weather swimming, and year-round hiking on woodland trails. The park's seventy-two camp sites ($8 a night) have electricity, water, hot showers, and rest rooms; 36 rustic but very snug cottages, by the lake and in the adjacent woodlands, are equipped down to sheets, towels, pots, and pans, at $45 a night Sunday through Thursday, $55 Friday and Saturday. The park office is open 8:00 A.M. to 5:00 P.M. Contact Vogel State Park, Blairsville 30512, (404) 745–2628.

There's also excellent fishing, swimming, boating, and picnicking in nearby Lake Winfield Scott, a U.S. Forest Service recreation area, (404) 745–6928.

Habersham County

Habersham County claims some of northeast Georgia's most photogenic Blue Ridge Mountain country. These mountains and valleys, thousands of acres of Chattahoochee National Forest, and scores of lakes and streams offer limitless opportunities to take a hike, ride a bike, camp out, and fish, swim, and otherwise unwind.

Habersham is one of Georgia's major apple producers. Rich soil and a cool climate encouraged English and Canadian families to initiate the apple-growing arts here in the 1920s. In October, roadside stands overflow with Red Delicious, Stayman Winesaps, dark red Yates, and bright yellow-green Granny Smiths. You can buy 'em by the sackful or the carload and also purchase home-made apple jelly, apple butter, and ice-cold, freshly squeezed sweet apple cider by the glass and gallon jugful. As a rule, Habersham orchards don't allow visitors to come in and pick their own fruit.

Habersham County also produces enough grapes to merit location of one of Georgia's four major wineries. **Habersham Vineyards** (404–778–WINE) at Highways 365 and 441 near the small town of Baldwin, produces more than a dozen types of wine, including pinot blanc, chablis, chardonnay, riesling, and sauvignon. Habersham's Georgia muscadine wine has won gold medals in international competitions. Other wines have captured silver and bronze medals here and overseas.

You may tour the winery and enjoy free samples, Monday through Saturday 10:00 A.M. to 5:00 P.M. and Sunday 1:00 to 6:00 P.M.

Clarkesville, Habersham's snug little county seat, is a happy hunting grounds for antiques and mountain handicrafts. Several shops around the courthouse square on Highway 441 are loaded with handcrafted furniture, pottery, paintings, weaving, leather-work, handmade baskets and quilts, toys, dolls, jellies, jams, and preserves.

When all that browsing and decision-making saps your strength, go for a recharge at Taylor's Trolley (404–754–5566), a turn-of-the-century drugstore turned into a most attractive café. Owners Kathleen and James Taylor have recreated the old soda fountain feeling with ceiling fans, country antiques, and old-timey chairs and tables. The service area is behind the marble soda fountain. The menu includes fresh mountain trout, steaks, prime rib, homemade soups, salads, sandwiches, and desserts. Prices are inexpensive at lunch Monday through Saturday, and dinner Tuesday through Saturday. Taylor's Trolley is located on Highway 441 at the town square, Clarkesville 30523.

The Charm House Inn is Clarkesville's most dramatic landmark. The white-columned Greek Revival mansion sits on a tree-shaded knoll on Highway 441 at the southern end of town. You can dine in the large airy dining room or spend the night in rooms furnished with four-poster beds, rockers, and private baths. The dining room menu features baked ham, shrimp Newburg, fried chicken, quiche, and crepes. A bountiful buffet is served after noon on Sunday. Owners Mabel Fry and Rhea Allen will make you feel more like house guests than hotel guests. Double rooms with continental breakfast are $39 to $49. Contact the owners at P.O. Box 392, Clarkesville 30523, (404) 754–9347.

The Glen-Ella Springs Hotel sits on seventeen pastoral acres, off Highway 441/23 between Clarkesville and Tallulah Falls. Owners Barrie and Bobby Aycock have converted the one hundred-year-old hotel building into a sixteen-room country inn, full of rustic touches and modern conveniences. All the rooms have porches with rocking chairs, antiques, and heart-of-pine paneling. Some have fireplaces and whirlpools. The dining room features fresh mountain trout but varies from traditional mountain fare with veal dishes, lobster, and other American/continental entrées. Doubles are $60 to $75, suites $125. Contact the Aycocks, Route 3, Bear Gap Road, Clarkesville 30523; (404) 754–7295.

Highway 197, twisting and turning north between Clarkesville and Clayton, is one of north Georgia's prettiest drives. The **Mark of the Potter,** 9 miles north of Clarkesville, is a favorite stop for mountain visitors. The weathered old white frame corn-grinding mill, by the rapids of the Soque River, sells some of the finest work of Georgia's most accomplished crafts people. Shelves are laden with superb pottery, colorful fabrics, metal, and leatherwork.

Browsing inevitably will take you onto the porch overhanging the Soque to throw treats to the fat, pampered trout swimming in the river's pools. Mark of the Potter (404–947–3440) is open daily. If you follow Highway 197 another 8 miles north, you'll be at the dining room of LaPrade's, one of the mountains' most famous eateries (see "Rabun County"). Habersham also shares Tallulah Falls and Tallulah Gorge with Rabun County.

South of Clarkesville, the little town of Demorest, on Highway 441, is worth a visit. A couple of antique shops are on the short main street, and you may stroll the peaceful campus of Piedmont College.

Franklin, Hart and Stephens Counties

Created by U.S. Army Corps of Engineers impoundments of the Savannah River, Lake Hartwell is a vast inland sea, whose 56,000 acres offer virtually limitless off-the-beaten-path opportunities for fishing, boating, swimming, and nature hikes. You can headquarter at two state parks on the lake and play a nine-hole golf course at another park, away from the lake. While wandering the green and hilly backroads of Hart, Stephens, and Franklin counties, you can rest awhile at an eighteenth-century stagecoach inn and reminisce with old-timers who remember the fiery exploits of "The Georgia Peach," baseball's Ty Cobb.

Hart State Park, near the town of Hartwell, spreads 147 acres along the lakeshore. You can set up housekeeping in eighty-three tent and trailer sites, with electrical and water hookups, adjacent to showers and rest rooms ($8 a night), and in furnished cottages ($45 a night Sunday through Thursday, $55 Friday and Saturday), and indulge in swimming, boating, waterskiing, and fishing for largemouth bass, black crappie, bream, rainbow trout, and walleye pike. You can angle from fishing docks or find your own favorite spot away from the competition. Contact park superintendent, 1515 Hart Park Road, Hartwell 30643, (404) 376–8756.

Situated on a wooded peninsula jutting into Lake Hartwell, **Tugaloo State Park,** near Lavonia, is another motherlode of largemouth bass and other fish fry favorites. Nonfisherfolk can play tennis and miniature golf, swim and waterski from a sand beach, and hike and bike on trails threading through the surrounding woodlands. Lodgings include twenty furnished cottages and 122 tent and trailer sites. Contact park superintendent, Route 1, Lavonia 30553, (404) 356–4362.

If you've been driving all day, tantalized by thoughts of a round of golf, a swim, maybe even some late-afternoon fishing, **Victo-**

ria Bryant State Park may be the answer to your prayers. This scenic 406-acre park, off Interstate 85 near Royston, invites you to challenge its 3,288-yard, par 34, nine-hole golf course. It's hardly a monster, but clusters of Georgia pines, plenty of hills and water will keep you on your toes. Rental clubs and pull carts are available at the clubhouse, which also has changing rooms and showers and a snack bar with light refreshments.

Non-golfers can splash in the swimming pool and angle for bream, brass, and catfish in the stocked pond. Victoria Bryant's twenty-five camping sites ($8 a night) have electrical and water hookups and access to showers and rest rooms. Contact park superintendent, Route 1, Royston 30662, (404) 245–6270.

If you're a baseball buff, drive down to Royston and see the little town that gave the world "The Georgia Peach." Some gloves and bats, plaques, newspaper clippings, and other memorabilia are displayed at city hall. If you drop by the Roystonian Café, on Highway 29 at the southern edge of town, (404) 245–7243, you might have a cup of coffee with a long-time resident who remembers when Tyrus Raymond "Ty" Cobb was the terror of the American League and one of the greatest players in baseball history.

In the 1830s and '40s—about a century before Ty Cobb headed for the majors—travelers suffering the bone-jarring stagecoach journey through the northeast Georgia wilderness took solace in the thought that by and by they'd reach **Travelers Rest,** near Toccoa.

The sturdy, two-story, fourteen-room plank structure was built in 1833 as the plantation home of wealthy planter Devereaux Jarrett. As more and more travelers streamed through the region, the enterprising Jarrett added onto the house and turned it into a nineteenth-century bed and breakfast. South Carolina statesman John C. Calhoun was once a guest, and Joseph E. Brown, Georgia's Civil War governor, spent his honeymoon here.

Maintained by the Georgia Department of Natural Resources, the fourteen rooms are still rich with four-poster beds, rocking chairs, vanities, marble-topped tables, goose feather mattresses, spinning wheels, china, cutlery and glassware, and memorabilia of Travelers Rest's days as a post office. The grounds are shaded by a huge white oak tree, believed to be well into its third century and several one hundred-year-old crepe myrtles.

Off Highway 123, 6 miles northeast of Toccoa, Travelers Rest (404–886–2256) is open Tuesday through Saturday 9:00 A.M.

to 5:00 P.M. and Sunday 2:00 to 5:30 P.M. Adults are $1; ages five to twelve, 50¢; under five, free.

Visitors are invited to relax by **Toccoa Falls,** a 186-foot cataract on the campus of Toccoa Falls College. A path leads to a rock wall behind the falls; another leads to a rustic stairway to the top of the falls. All is peaceful now, but on November 7, 1977, an earthen dam above the falls collapsed, sending torrents of water across the campus and claiming many lives. The dam was never replaced. The campus is on Highway 17, on the northwest side of Toccoa, a town of 10,000, near Lake Hartwell and the Georgia–South Carolina border.

White County

When your children pose that age-old question—"Where do babies come from?"—take them to Cleveland and show them. At Cleveland's **Babyland General Hospital** (404–865–2171) some very special "babies" come from a cabbage patch. Originally a doctor's turn-of-the-century clinic, the white frame "hospital" at 19 Underwood Street/Highway 129 is where the soft-sculptured Cabbage Patch Kids, created by White County's own Xavier Roberts, first see day's light. Uniformed "nurses" lead you through the nursery, day care center, and delivery room. At the magic moment, a "doctor" in surgical garb plucks a new-born Kid from a patch of sculptured cabbage leaves to "oohs" and "aahs" all around. You can take home a cuddly Cabbage Patch Kid of your very own. Just remember, they're "babies," not "dolls"; not "bought," but "adopted." The hospital is open Monday through Saturday 8:30 A.M. to 5:00 P.M. and Sunday 1:00 to 5:00 P.M.

Xavier Robert's rich imagination has created the Blue Ridge country's most exotic, and unusual, lodgings. Departing totally from traditional mountain architecture, Villagio di Montagna seems more like a French or Italian import. Nestled among the trees and hills, Villagio's Mediterranean/Art Deco buildings are a muted mauve color, with ample use of tiles, marble, and glass blocks. Guest rooms have service bars and refrigerators, private balconies, fireplaces, and satellite television. Guests may while away their days at the swimming pool, tropical gardens, a rock garden Jacuzzi, and a spa with whirlpool, steam room, and sauna. Doubles are $100 to $120. Contact P.O. Box 714, Cleveland

30528, (404) 865–7000.

Cleveland's town square has lots of place to buy pottery, weaving, paintings, and other mountain handicrafts. For a taste of the mountains, head for Lagniappe (404–865–5504) and the Mauney House (404–865–4011).

If the sheer granite escarpments of **Mount Yonah,** off Highway 75 north of Cleveland, set your rock-climbing juices flowing, make plans to scale the heights with commercial outfitters in Atlanta. Xanadu Mountaineering (404–257–0600) and High Country Outfitters (404–952–8562) will put you in the proper climbing gear and send you up Yonah's 150- to 300-foot cliffs with experienced guides. Mount Yonah is also one of Georgia's best and most popular hang-gliding points.

Driving up to the **Old Sautee Store** (404–878–2281) at the junction of Highways 17 and 255, you might imagine an old-time mercantile stocked with bolts of cloth, seeds, farm implements, and sacks of cornmeal. Walk inside and what do your wondering eyes behold, but an array of tempting goods from Scandinavia: Norwegian and Icelandic sweaters, jackets and coats; crystal, dinnerware, needlework, gourmet foods, jewelry, and unique gifts from Sweden, Denmark, and Finland. On special occasions, owner Astrid Fried appears in her ornate Norwegian wedding dress. The adjacent log cabin sells Christmas ornaments the year round. The store is open daily.

Practically next door to the Old Sautee Store, the Sautee Inn (404–878–2940) is a charming place to relax and enjoy excellent Southern and international cooking. The restaurant is housed in a turn-of-the-century summer hotel. Service is buffet style, and afterward you may sit a spell in the front porch rockers. It's open daily.

You can also spread a picnic by the **Stovall Covered Bridge,** in a small park by Chickamauga Creek on Highway 255. Only thirty-three feet long, the bridge is one of the shortest anywhere in Georgia.

The Stovall House, nearby on Highway 255, is one of the nicest country inns anywhere in the state. Built in 1837, the handsome two-story frame house was purchased in 1982 by Atlantans Ham and Kathy Schwartz. Their love of their adopted mountain home is reflected in five guest rooms decorated with country antiques and all the modern comforts. Their dining room features Southern and continental cooking and is one of the best anywhere in the mountains. For pure, sweet relaxation, settle yourself into a porch swing and listen to the absolute peace of this lovely countryside. Rates are about $60 double. Contact the Stovall House, Route 1, Box 103-A, Sautee 30571, (404) 878–3355.

Highway 17 cuts a most picturesque path through the Sautee-Nacoochee Valley as it meanders westerly toward Helen. You may want to stop for a picture—or attend Sunday services—at Crescent Hill Baptist Church, on a wooded hillock near the intersection of Highways 17 and 75. The pretty Carpenter Gothic church was built in the 1870s by the same well-off gentleman who built the grand Victorian house and gazebo atop the Indian mound at Highways 17 and 75.

Going north on combined Highway 17/75, stop off at Nora Mill Granary & Store (404–878–2927). Founded in 1876 on the banks of the Chattahoochee River, the mill's current owners still grind corn into meal and grits in the tried and true old-fashioned way. It's open daily.

Don't try to pinch yourself awake as you drive by the "Wilkommen" signs, welcoming you to **"Alpine Helen."** You haven't wandered onto a Disney film set. About twenty years ago, this then-humble mountain hamlet underwent a wholesale transformation into a make-believe Alpine village. Nowadays, the red-tile roofs, flower boxes, biergartens, and stucco-fronted shops selling cuckoo clocks, Christmas ornaments, Tyrolean hats, and loden coats put the once-quiet village very much on the well-beaten path. Like it or disdain it, Helen's worth at least a short stroll and a browse. The many inns and "hofs" around town are good bases for more off-the-beaten-path adventures, such as the Appalachian Trail, Richard Russell Scenic Highway, and Chattahoochee National Forest. In trout season, you can don your waders and cast in the Chattahoochee River, which rises near here and wends its bonny way through the middle of town.

More Blue Ridge than Bavarian, Betty's Country Store (404–878–2943), on the north end of town, is a fun place to look around. The rustic store is loaded with jams and jellies, fresh vegetables, gourds, cookbooks, canned goods, cheeses, gourmet coffee, apple cider, and other goods. The café area in the back serves a hearty breakfast, and great chili, sandwiches, and desserts. It's open every day.

If you've never made it to Munich for Oktoberfest, Helen has a scaled-down replica. In late September and early October, the town's pavilion resounds to oompah bands and thousands of folk-dancing feet. In late October and early November, the mountain hardwoods change their colors as brilliantly as those in New England, making this an especially worthwhile time to visit. It's also prime season for freshly squeezed apple cider and boiled peanuts. Simmered in brine, in huge iron kettles, the goobers are warm, salty, sticky, and a special mountain delicacy that not everyone goes for, but that should at least be experienced.

Unicoi State Park, just north of Helen, is a treat that everyone can enjoy. With 1,081 acres of highlands and woodlands, threaded by streams, lakes, and waterfalls, there's plenty of off-the-beaten-path solitude.

Swimming, canoeing, and fishing focus on a picture-postcard fifty-three-acre lake. You may take solitary walks on 12 miles of trails and take part in nature walks led by park naturalists. Craftsmen share the secrets of pottery, quilting, dulcimer- and furniture-making, and other mountain arts. The handicraft shop in the Unicoi Lodge sells an array of beautiful items.

Also in the lodge, the cafeteria-style dining room serves excellent breakfast, lunch, and dinner at extremely low prices. The park's accommodations include ninety-six camping sites, with water, electricity, nearby showers, and rest rooms ($8), and two- and three-bedroom, completely furnished cottages, $45 to $65 a night. Contact park superintendent, P.O. Box 849, Helen 30545, (404) 878–2824.

Anna Ruby Falls is the awesome showpiece of a 1,600-acre Chattahoochee National Forest recreation area that neighbors Unicoi. From the parking area, follow a moderately strenuous half-mile trail through the woodlands bordering a swift-flowing stream. An observation platform sits at the base of Anna Ruby's two cascades, dropping dramatically 153 and 50 feet over the edge of Tray Mountain. Back at the parking area, restore your energy with a picnic by the water's edge.

Lumpkin County

In 1828, a trapper named Benjamin Parks allegedly stubbed his toe on a rock in Dahlonega and shouted the north Georgia version of "Eureka!" as he gazed at a vein of gold that soon sent prospectors streaming into these hills. *Dahlonega* is a Cherokee

Indian word meaning "precious yellow," and until the War Between the States, the substance flowed into a major U.S. Mint right here. Although it's no longer a major industry, enough gold is still mined to periodically releaf the dome of Georgia's state capitol and intrigue visitors who pan for it at reconstructed camps.

True to its heritage, the **Dahlonega Courthouse Gold Museum,** in the center of the little town of 2,800, chronicles the gold rush and the numerous mines that flourished in these parts. A twenty-eight-minute film upstairs in the old courtroom is especially worthwhile. Operated by the Georgia Department of Natural Resources, the Gold Museum, Dahlonega 30533, (404) 864–2257, is open Tuesday through Saturday 9:00 A.M. to 5:00 P.M. and Sunday 2:00 to 5:30 P.M. Adults are $1.50; ages six to twelve, 75¢; under age six, no charge.

Buildings around the square have a rustic frontier look. Shops purvey gold-panning equipment, ice cream, fudge, mountain handicrafts, gold jewelry, and antiques. Many people make the 70-mile drive north from Atlanta just to feast at the famous Smith House. Off the square at 202 South Chestatee Street, Dahlonega 30533, (404) 864–3566. The Smith House puts out huge family-style spreads with fried chicken, chicken and dumplings, beef stew, shrimp, numerous vegetables, biscuits, relishes, and dessert for about $10 a person. They also serve breakfast and have a cafeteria line for those not up to the full board. It's open daily except Monday.

The Worley Homestead, a block off the square at 410 West Main Street, Dahlonega 30533, (404) 864–7002, is one of the mountain country's most charming bed and breakfasts. Seven guest rooms and an adjacent cottage are decorated with four-poster beds and other antique furnishings. Rates of $50 to $70 double include a monumental Southern breakfast, with home-made biscuits and syrup, sausage, eggs, grits, and gravy. Afterwards, you may want to walk around the neighboring North Georgia College campus. The administration building tower is leafed with local gold.

Gold Rush Days, the third weekend of October, celebrate the gilded heritage with arts and crafts, clog dancing, and lots of bluegrass fiddling and singing. You can pan for gold the year round at **Crisson's Mine,** Wimpy Mill Road, Dahlonega 30533. You'll feel some of old Benjamin Park's excitement and might even whoop out "Eureka!" when you spot a few grains gleaming amid the mud in your pan.

Dahlonega is a popular gateway to the northeast Georgia mountain vacation areas. From here, Highway 19 snakes north toward Vogel State Park, while other roads aim toward Helen, Cleveland, and Amicalola State Park.

Contact Dahlonega–Lumpkin County Chamber of Commerce, P.O. Box 2037, Dahlonega 30533, (404) 864–3711.

Pickens County

Two of north Georgia's most interesting and unusual dining and lodging places are off the beaten path, among the green hills and marble quarries of Pickens County. The Woodbridge Inn at Jasper and the Tate House at Tate depart joyously and deliciously from the culinary path most often trod in rural Georgia.

German-born Joe Rueffert and his Georgia-born wife Brenda have been the hospitable proprietors of the Woodbridge Inn for about a dozen years. On the surface, the rustic pre–Civil War inn, with the checkered tablecloths and big windows with panoramic views of the mountains, gives few hints of surprises. It's only when Joe dons his chef's hat and parades from the kitchen with grilled swordfish steaks, fresh grouper, and mahi-mahi with rich creamy sauces; chateaubriand *forestiere* and steak *au poivre;* veal dishes with silken bearnaise and hollandaise sauces; roast duckling with orange sauce; bananas Foster and other luscious desserts that the wealth of this "find" finally sinks in.

You may select American and European wines and beers from the Woodbridge list or brown-bag your own spirits. After your feast, you're only a few steps from your lodgings in the inn's chalet-style rooms. Comfortably furnished and air-conditioned, the large rooms come with complimentary mountain views for $40 to $65. The dining room serves lunch on Sunday and dinner Tuesday through Saturday. Prices are moderate, and major credit cards are accepted. Contact Woodbridge Inn, 411 Chambers Street, Jasper 30143, (404) 692–6293.

The inn is, true to its name, across a wooden bridge, at the northern edge of the bucolic small town of Jasper. If you've forgotten how sweet and peaceful a town of 5,000 can be, take a leisurely constitutional on Jasper's main street, and chat with the folks in the stores and around the Pickens County Courthouse. The Ruefferts don't serve breakfast, so you may wish to indulge in the grits and eggs at one of Jasper's hometown cafés.

The Tate House, also known as "The Pink Marble Mansion," was built in the early 1920s with rare Etowah pink marble taken from the neighboring quarries. The Great Depression dealt harshly with the Tate family, owners of the quarries and the mansion. The classical-style mansion sat vacant from the late 1930s until 1974, when it was rediscovered by Mrs. Ann Laird, who has diligently and lovingly turned it into a showplace of northeast Georgia hospitality.

Many people drive up from Atlanta and from across the mountain country to enjoy lunch, dinner, or Sunday brunch in these beautiful rooms. Lunch, Wednesday through Saturday, is highlighted by chicken Marsala, roast pork loin with escalloped apples, and deluxe sandwiches and salads. Dinner, Wednesday through Saturday, features fresh seafoods, veal and lamb, chateaubriand and prime ribs. For Sunday brunch, you may indulge in Belgian waffles, omelets, prime ribs and chicken dishes. Wine and beer are available. Prices range from inexpensive to expensive. Credit cards are accepted.

Overnight accommodations include nine deluxe log cabins with hot tubs and fireplaces and four suites in the mansion itself. Rates are about $105 to $140 a night. Contact Tate House, P.O. Box 33, Tate 30177, (404) 735–3122, toll-free in Georgia (800) 342–7515. Tate is on Highway 53.

A driving tour of Pickens County is a nice way to spend a day. John's Mill, a nineteenth-century water-powered mill, is a picturesque place to picnic and to buy a sackful of stone-ground cornmeal. From the junction of Highway 53 and Interstate 575, drive west on Highway 53 about 7 miles and turn right on the road between the Hinton Milling Co. and a service station. Continue $1/4$-mile to the John's Mill sign, turn left; the log cabin mill and stone dam are at the bottom of the hill. There's no phone, but the mill is usually in operation on weekdays and Saturdays.

Amicalola Falls State Park and the **Appalachian Trail approach trail** are a scenic half-hour drive from Jasper, in neighboring Dawson County. The Appalachian Trail is described at the beginning of this chapter.

Hall County

The mountain may not have come to Mohammed, as the old saying goes, but in 1957, an inland sea came to northeast Georgia's Hall County. The U.S. Army Corps of Engineers closed the Buford Dam on the Chattahoochee River and created Lake Sidney Lanier. Nowadays, about 25,000 of the lake's 38,000 acres and some 380 miles of its green and hilly 550-mile shoreline cover former Hall County farmlands and forests.

State-operated **Lake Lanier Islands,** the lake's major recreational mecca, is an attractively maintained spread of golf and tennis, horseback riding, swimming beaches, marinas with boat rentals, a resort hotel, campgrounds, and furnished cottages. During the off seasons when the swimming beaches are closed and on most weekdays throughout the year, there are plenty of places to get off the beaten track. Contact Lanier Islands, Box 605, Buford 30518, (404) 945–6701; U.S. Army Corps of Engineers, 30 Pryor Street, Atlanta 30303, (404) 945–9531; and the Gainesville–Hall County Tourism and Convention Bureau, P.O. Box 374, Gainesville 30503, (404) 536–6206.

At the end of a big day of fishing, boating, and swimming, join famished natives at Major McGill's Fish House, an unpretentious and always busy set of dining rooms in the small community of Flowery Branch, on Highway 13, (404) 967–6001. Specialties are fried and broiled Lake Lanier catfish, oysters, shrimp, mountain trout, steaks, and chicken.

Gainesville, the Hall County seat (population about 25,000), is a popular gateway to the northeast Georgia vacationlands. Before heading for the hills, enjoy a leisurely stroll through the **Green Street Historical District.** The wide, tree-lined thoroughfare, also designated as Highway 129, holds a wealth of late–nineteenth-and early–twentieth-century Victorian and Neoclassical Revival residences. You may dine in one and stay overnight in another. Rudolph's On Green Street, 700 Green Street, (404) 534–2226, is a baronial English Tudor rich with dark, exposed beams, stained-glass windows, Oriental carpets, and Duncan Phyfe furnishings. Lunch and dinner entrées are equally impressive: broiled baby salmon, chicken Florentine, roast duckling, several veal dishes, and Georgia mountain trout, complemented by wines from California, Georgia, and Europe. You may also have a hamburger, salads, and a simple breakfast or eggs Benedict. Prices range from inexpensive to expensive, and major cards are accepted.

The Dunlap House, practically next door to Rudolph's at 635 Green Street, Gainesville 30501, (404) 536–0200, is a gracious 1910 mansion with twelve guest rooms at about $65 double.

Also in the Green Street Historical District, the Quinlan Art Center (404–536–2575) shows the works of state, regional, and national artists Monday through Saturday 10:00 A.M. to 4:00 P.M. and Sundays 2:00 to 5:00 P.M. at no charge.

Green Street Station (404–534–6080) houses a Georgia mountains historical exhibit, permanent collection of mountain arts and crafts, and cartoons and memorabilia of Gainesville's Ed Dodd, creator of the "Mark Trail" comic strip. There's also a gift shop where you may purchase high-quality quilts, pottery, cookbooks, and other Appalachian crafts. It's open Monday through Saturday 10:00 A.M. to 4:00 P.M. and Sundays 2:00 to 5:00 P.M., no charge.

All the buildings around Roosevelt Square, in the center of Gainesville, have a distinctive 1930s Art Deco look. That's because all the older buildings in the area were lost, along with many lives, in a monster tornado in 1936. President Franklin D. Roosevelt's "New Deal" programs rebuilt the devastated town, and he spoke here at dedication ceremonies in 1938.

If you enjoy unusual monuments, bring your camera to Poultry Park, where a rooster atop a granite obelisk hails Gainesville's distinction as "Poultry Capital of the World." Some 2.6-million broilers leave here every week for kitchens around the world.

Clarke County

Antebellum Athens throbs to the contemporary rhythms of 30,000 University of Georgia students who nearly equal "The Classic City's" 42,000 "townies." Founded in 1785, America's oldest chartered state university didn't convene its first classes until 1801. That same year, Athens was founded on a hill above the Oconee River and named for Greece's hub of classical learning. Planters and literati embellished the campus and Athens' elm- and oak-lined thoroughfares with outstanding examples of Greek Revival, Georgian, and Federal architecture. Over the ensuing decades, "town and gown" have coexisted in peace and harmony that's only seriously disrupted when 80,000 UGA "Bulldog" football fanatics shake the skies over Sanford Stadium with exhortations of "Go-ooo Dawgs!"

Start your visit at the Athens Welcome Center, in the Church-

Waddel-Brumby House, 280 East Dougherty Street, (404) 546–1805. The fine Federalist house was built in 1820 for Alonzo Church, who later became UGA's president. It's believed to be the city's oldest surviving residence. You may tour the lovely rooms and pick up information about other attractions and tours. It's open Monday through Saturday 9:00 A.M. to 5:00 P.M. and Sunday 2:00 to 5:00 P.M.

Athens of Old Tours (404–549–6800), led by Athens Convention and Visitors Bureau guides, take you through antebellum homes, gardens, and attractions around the city and university campus. You may also pick up a walking-driving tour map at the Welcome Center and see Athens at your own pace.

The Taylor-Grady House, 634 Prince Avenue, (404) 549–8688, was built in 1845. The thirteen Doric columns surrounding three sides of the Greek Revival showplace allegedly represent the original thirteen colonies, bound in a Union, just as the columns were bound by a wrought-iron railing. Now owned by the city of Athens, the rooms are filled with period antiques and open to the public Monday through Friday 10:00 A.M. to 3:30 P.M. Admission is $2.50.

Other classical residences that may be viewed from the outside include the University of Georgia president's home, a regal Greek Revival with fourteen Corinthian columns on the front and sides, and a parade of Doric columns facing a five-acre garden at the rear. It's in elite company at 570 Prince Avenue.

Civil War buffs shouldn't miss the "Double-Barreled Cannon," a whimsical piece of memorabilia that was a spectacular failure. Cast in Athens in 1862, each barrel was to be loaded with cannonballs connected to each other by an eight-foot chain. When fired, the missiles were *supposed* to exit together, pull the chain tight, and sweep across the battlefield like a scythe. In reality, the barrels weren't synchronized, and instead of devastating Yankees, the errant shots plowed up a field, knocked down trees, and killed a cow. The beloved curiosity is now the centerpiece of a pretty downtown park. "The Tree That Owns Itself" is another one-of-a-kind landmark. The fifty-foot oak, at Dearing and Findley streets, was granted its autonomy and eight feet of land on all sides by a UGA professor many years ago.

The UGA campus is a treasury of classical and contemporary architecture. According to tradition, freshmen are forbidden to walk through the University Arch, which dates to 1857 and leads to the stately old trees and venerable buildings of historic North Campus. Listed on the National Register of Historic Places, "Old North's" dowagers include Phi Kappa Hall, an 1836 Greek Revival; Federal-style Waddel Hall, 1820; Palladian style Demosthenian Hall, 1824; Greek Revival University Chapel, whose bells joyously proclaim "Bulldog" football triumphs; and Old College, where in 1832 Crawford W. Long, a Georgian who'd later discover the use of anesthesia for surgery, roomed with Alexander Hamilton Stephens, who became vice-president of the Confederacy.

Elsewhere on the huge, sprawling campus, the Georgia Museum of Art's permanent collections include over 5,000 paintings, drawings and sculpture by nineteenth- and twentieth-century American artists. Many important traveling exhibitions also stop here. The galleries are open Monday through Saturday, free of charge.

Flower and garden lovers should allot plenty of time for the **State Botanical Garden.** The 293-acre preserve of gardens, nature trails, a visitors center and state-of-the-art conservatory contains thousands of native and exotic plants, large stands of trees, and small populations of white-tailed deer, raccoons, rabbits, and many species of birds. The visitors center/conservatory is open Monday through Saturday 9:00 A.M. to 4:30 P.M. and Sunday 11:30 A.M. to 4:30 P.M. The outdoor gardens and nature trails are open daily 8:00 A.M. to dusk. Lunch is served daily in the Garden Café, 2450 South Milledge Avenue, (404) 542–1244.

With all these thousands of perpetually ravenous students, finding a place to eat is no problem. For food-on-the-run, try the chili dogs, burgers, fries, sandwiches, and ice cream at the Varsity, 1000 West Broad Street (404–548–7160). At the loftier end of the culinary spectrum, Martell's serves elegant French and continental cuisine and wines in antebellum mansion at 295 East Dougherty Street (404) 353–8387. Students and "townies" will be glad to direct you to their favorite places.

Two bed-and-breakfast inns are perfect complements to Athens' antebellum landmarks. The Old Winterville Inn, in a quiet village on Highway 78/Lexington Road, 7 miles east of Athens, dates back to the 1870s when it thrived as a traveling salesmen's hotel. Current owners Don and Julie Bower have restored the original board-and-batten clapboard exterior and the interior heart pine floors and hand-planed plank walls. Guest rooms have a bedroom, sitting room, kitchen, and private entrance and are

$46 a double. It's at 108 South Main Street, Winterville 30683, (404) 742–7340.

Book in advance if you're coming in June for Winterville's annual Marigold Festival.

The Hardeman/Hutchens House, 5355 Lexington Road/Highway 78, Athens 30605, (404) 353–1855, is a pre–Civil War house restored by Paul and Jane Hutchens. Rates of $35 include a full Southern breakfast.

In case you believe New England has a monopoly on covered bridges, **Watson Mill Bridge State Park** will be a pleasant surprise. Off Highway 22 east of Athens, the 144-acre park is the site of Georgia's longest covered bridge. Four spans of the century-old wooden bridge stretch 236 feet across the South Fork of the Broad River. It's an idyllic spot for a picnic, canoeing, and an overnight stay in the campground ($8 a night). Contact park superintendent, Route 1, Comer 30629, (404) 783–5349.

Athens is the northern anchor of "The Antebellum Trail," an association of historic towns along Highway 441 in east-central Georgia. See other chapters on Baldwin, Jones, Putnam, and Morgan counties.

Barrow County

Approaching the Winder/Chestnut Mountain exit (#48) on Interstate 85 northeast of Atlanta, what appears to be a sixteenth-century French castle, surrounded by neatly laid out vineyards, rises from the piny landscape. That's no mirage. Established in the early 1980s, **Chateau Elan Winery** was Georgia's first major new winery since the end of Prohibition. Inside Chateau Elan's turreted "castle," you're welcome to stroll a movie-set French marketplace and purchase jams, mustards, wine guides, cookbooks, picnic hampers, wine coolers, and other gifts. A pictorial display explains the history of wine and the wine-making process.

Before purchasing the Chateau's grape, you'll want to have a free tasting. In a very short time, Chateau Elan's chardonnay, riesling, cabernet sauvignon, zinfandel, and other varieties have captured more than fifty-five awards in national competitions. Southerners are especially partial to the sweet and fruity Summerwine, a blend of peaches and muscadine grapes. Wines are about $5 to $10 a bottle.

A sidewalk café (404–867–8200) inside the marketplace serves light lunches with quiche, pâtés, chicken breast, salads, cheeses, and Friday and Saturday evening five-course dinners with wines. You may also purchase picnic baskets and sit outdoors by the vineyards. It's open daily.

Barrow County's second winery opened in late 1988. Chestnut Mountain Winery (404–867–6914), also off Interstate 85's exit 48, offers free tours and tastings in a farm warehouse refashioned to resemble a medieval castle. The winery is surrounded by thirty acres of woodlands and rose gardens, and visitors are welcome to bring a picnic lunch. Hours are 10:00 A.M. until dark, Monday through Saturday, and 12:30 to 6:00 P.M. on Sunday. Write Box 72, Braselton 30517.

If you always wanted to own your own town, go to exit 49 and inquire at the general mercantile store in the little community of Braselton. The mercantile, a furniture store, supermarket, bank, post office, about twenty houses and industrial park, a café, a mill building, and everything else hereabouts is owned by the Braselton family, which has been looking for a buyer for the past decade or so. The price is reputedly negotiable, but so far no one has come up with just the right one.

If all you're looking for is bed-and-breakfast lodgings off the beaten path, there's a room reserved for you at the Hill House Inn (404–654–3425) at neighboring Hoschton. The stately two-story Neoclassical brick home has been nestled into a pecan grove since 1913. The interior is rich with mahogany. Four guest rooms are furnished with antiques. Guests customarily awaken to the aroma of freshly baked pecan pastries. In cool weather, owners and guests gather at the library fireplace and in the summer lounge on the spacious front porch. Doubles are $60. Contact Dennis Pitters, Hill House Inn, Hoschton, 30548.

Fort Yargo State Park, at nearby Winder, takes its name from a still-standing log blockhouse white settlers built in 1792 as protection against hostile Creeks and Cherokees. It's an inviting place to swim, fish, rent paddleboats, row boats, and canoes on a big green lake. You can also enjoy tennis and miniature golf, hike nature trails, and set the youngsters loose on the playground. Will-A-Way Recreation Area, inside the park, has facilities for handicapped persons, including specially equipped, furnished cottages. There are also furnished cottages and camp sites not so equipped. Contact the park superintendent, Winder 30680, (404) 867–3489.

Northeast Georgia

At Christmas season, many people bring their holiday mail to the post office in the nearby little community of Bethlehem for that special postmark.

Index

Index

About the Author

William Schemmel is a full-time freelance writer and photographer who travels from Paris, Texas, to Paris, France, but most enjoys telling others about his native state of Georgia. His work appears regularly in *Travel Holiday* magazine, *National Geographic Traveler, Modern Bride, Atlanta Journal-Constitution, Chicago Tribune, San Juan Star,* and numerous other magazines, newspapers and guidebooks. A member of the Society of American Travel Writers, he has experienced adventures on Georgia's off-the-beaten paths for more than twenty-five years. He invites you to get off the interstate highways and make your own fascinating discoveries.